Collins

AQA

GCSE

PHYSICS

SET A – Paper 1 Higher Tier

Author: Lynn Pharaoh

H

Time allowed: 1 hour 45 minutes

Materials

For this paper you must have:

- a ruler
- a calculator
- the Physics Equation Sheet (found at the end of the paper).

Instructions

- Answer **all** questions in the spaces provided.
- Do all rough work in this book. Cross through any work you do not want to be marked.

Information

- There are 100 marks available on this paper.
- The marks for questions are shown in brackets.
- You are expected to use a calculator where appropriate.
- You are reminded of the need for good English and clear presentation in your answers.
- When answering questions 02.1, 04.2 and 09.1 you need to make sure that your answer:
  - is clear, logical, sensibly structured
  - fully meets the requirements of the question
  - shows that each separate point or step supports the overall answer.

Advice

- In all calculations, show clearly how you work out your answer.

Name: ....

01.1 Which type of radiation has a **range of a few metres in air**?

Tick **one** box.

Alpha ☐

Beta ☐

Gamma ☐

[1 mark]

01.2 Alpha radiation is described as having the highest **ionising power**.

Describe what is meant by **ionising power**.

State how the high ionising power of alpha radiation is linked to its range through the human body.

....

....

....

....

[3 marks]

01.3 A radioactive isotope emitting gamma radiation can be used as a tracer in medical diagnosis.

A gamma camera outside the human body then produces an image of the internal organ.

Explain why gamma radiation is suitable for this use.

_____

_____ **[1 mark]**

01.4 Which is the most suitable half-life for an isotope used as a tracer in medical diagnosis?

Tick **one** box.

10 seconds ☐

6 hours ☐

3 months ☐   **[1 mark]**

Explain your answer.

_____

_____

_____

_____ **[2 marks]**

02.1 A student is provided with the apparatus shown in **Figure 2.1**

Figure 2.1

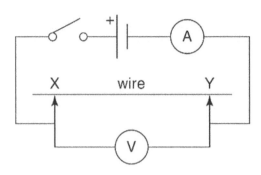

Describe how the student could use the apparatus in **Figure 2.1** to obtain accurate values of resistance for a range of different lengths of wire.

The wire is connected between crocodile clips X and Y.

....

....

....

....

....

....

....

....

[4 marks]

02.2 After the experiment, the student realised that the metre rule had been damaged at one end.

Instead of starting at 0 mm, the end of the rule corresponded to the 1 mm mark.

State what type of error this creates in the measurement of the wire's length.

_____ **[1 mark]**

02.3 Explain how the student should correct the length measurements made in the experiment.

_____

_____ **[1 mark]**

02.4 The resistance of the student's wire doubles each time the length connected between X and Y is doubled.

Sketch a graph on the axes in **Figure 2.2** to show how the resistance of the wire depends on its length.

Figure 2.2

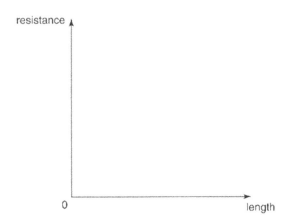

[1 mark]

Question 2 continues on the next page

02.5 **Figure 2.3** shows how the resistance of a 1 m length of nickel-chromium wire depends on the wire's **thickness**.

Figure 2.3

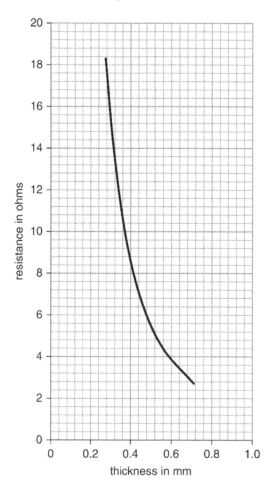

Give **one** conclusion based on the graph.

....

.... **[1 mark]**

02.6 Use **Figure 2.3** to estimate the resistance of a nickel-chromium wire of thickness 0.8 mm

Resistance = ... Ω   **[1 mark]**

03.1 An electric kettle is used to heat 1.0 kg of water.

Calculate the thermal energy that must be transferred to the water to raise its temperature from 20°C to 100°C

Specific heat capacity of water = 4200 J/ kg °C

Select the correct equation from the Physics Equation Sheet.

Thermal energy transferred = ... J [2 marks]

03.2 Write down the equation that links energy transferred, power and time.

.... [1 mark]

03.3 The electrical heater inside the kettle has a power of 3000 W

The kettle takes 120 s to bring the water to its boiling point.

Calculate the thermal energy transferred by the heater in the time taken to boil the water.

Thermal energy transferred = ... J [2 marks]

03.4 Write down the equation for efficiency.

.... [1 mark]

Question 3 continues on the next page

03.5 Calculate the efficiency of the kettle.

Give your answer as a percentage to 2 significant figures.

_____

_____

Efficiency = _____ % **[3 marks]**

03.6 The kettle is not 100% efficient, partly because thermal energy is dissipated to the surrounding room.

Suggest **one** other reason that the kettle is not 100% efficient.

_____

_____ **[1 mark]**

04.1 Electricity is generated in the UK using both renewable and non-renewable energy sources.

Explain what is meant by a **renewable** energy source.

....

....

[1 mark]

04.2 Compare the use of wind turbines and nuclear power stations for generating electricity in the UK.

Include a comparison of their **reliability** and their **environmental effects**.

....

....

....

....

....

....

....

....

....

....

....

....

[6 marks]

Turn over >

5   In Rutherford's alpha particle scattering experiment, a beam of alpha particles was fired at gold foil.

05.1 Give an order of magnitude estimate for the diameter of a gold atom.

Diameter ~ _____ m   **[1 mark]**

05.2 Any change in direction of the alpha particles on hitting the gold foil was monitored.

Table 5.1 shows some typical results.

Table 5.1

Path followed by the alpha particles	Percentage of alpha particles
Continued undeflected in a straight line	>99%
Deflected by angles up to 90°	0.05%
Deflected by angles greater than 90°	0.013%

This alpha particle scattering experiment led to the nuclear model of the atom replacing the plum pudding model.

Use the results in **Table 5.1** to explain why the model had to be replaced.

_____

_____

_____

_____

[4 marks]

05.3 The symbol for the nucleus of a stable isotope of gold is $^{197}_{79}\text{Au}$

Describe the arrangement and numbers of the different subatomic particles in a gold atom.

_____

_____

_____

_____

[4 marks]

06.1 Radon is a radioactive gas that is emitted from some types of rock.

Radon gas is one of the main natural sources of background radiation.

Give **one** other **natural source** of background radiation.

.... **[1 mark]**

06.2 Radon gas can accumulate in buildings.

Radon nuclei decay by emitting alpha particles.

Explain the particular hazard created by a radon gas being present in a building.

....

....

....

.... **[3 marks]**

06.3 **Table 6.1** contains dose data due to radon gas.

Table 6.1

Location	Annual average dose due to radon, in mSv
Whole of UK	1.3
Cornwall, UK	6.9

[Data from Public Health England]

Calculate **how many times greater** the radiation dose due to radon gas is in Cornwall compared with the average across the UK.

....

Number of times greater = ... **[1 mark]**

Question 6 continues on the next page

06.4 **Figure 6.1** shows the changes in activity of a sample of radon-222 as time passes.

Figure 6.1

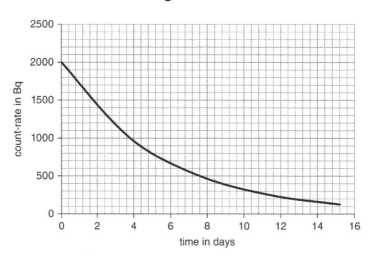

Use the graph to determine an accurate value for the half-life of radon-222

Show your working.

_____

_____

Half-life = _____ days **[3 marks]**

06.5 The activity of a sample of radon gas is measured at 400 kBq

Calculate how many days would have to pass for the activity of the sample to be less than 40 kBq

_____

_____

Number of days = _____ **[2 marks]**

06.6 The naturally occurring isotope of radon is $^{222}_{86}$Rn which decays by emitting an alpha particle to form polonium.

Complete the decay equation below:

$$^{222}_{86}\text{Rn} \rightarrow {}^{218}\text{Po} + {}^{4}\text{He}$$

[2 marks]

07.1 Name the system of cables and transformers that links power stations to consumers in the UK.

.... **[1 mark]**

07.2 Mains electricity supplies an alternating potential difference.

Explain what is meant by an **alternating** potential difference.

....

.... **[1 mark]**

07.3 In a faulty electric toaster, the live wire may make contact with the toaster's metal casing.

Explain why this could be very dangerous.

....

....

.... **[2 marks]**

07.4 There are three wires in the cable connecting a plug to a toaster.

Identify the wire that provides protection from the fault detailed in question 07.3

.... **[1 mark]**

07.5 An electric toaster has a power rating of 0.92 kW

The UK mains supplies a potential difference of 230 V

Calculate the electric current drawn by the toaster when it is plugged into the mains.

....

....

Current = ... A **[3 marks]**

Turn over >

08   **Figure 8.1** shows the circuit diagram for a torch.

Figure 8.1

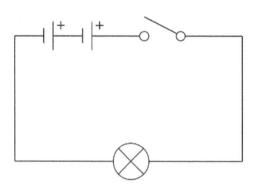

08.1 The battery supplies 3.0 V of potential difference across the bulb.

The resistance of the bulb is 100 Ω

Calculate the current flowing through the bulb.

Current = _____ A   **[3 marks]**

08.2 Calculate the charge that flows through the bulb if the torch is switched on for 5 minutes.

Charge = _____ C   **[3 marks]**

08.3 Calculate the energy transferred by the bulb over this 5 minutes.

Energy transferred = _____ J   **[2 marks]**

08.4 **Figure 8.2** shows three **identical** bulbs connected to a battery.

Figure 8.2

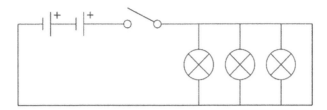

Which **two** statements about the circuit in **Figure 8.2** are correct?

Tick **two** boxes.

The potential difference across each bulb has the same value. ☐

The bulbs are connected in series. ☐

The current through each bulb has a different value. ☐

The bulbs are connected in parallel. ☐ **[2 marks]**

08.5 **Figure 8.3** shows three **different** bulbs connected to a battery.

Figure 8.3

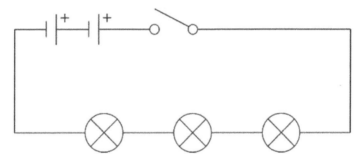

Bulbs A, B and C each have a **different** resistance value and **different** brightness.

Which **two** statements about the circuit are correct?

Tick **two** boxes.

The potential difference across each bulb has the same value. ☐

The bulbs are connected in series. ☐

The current through each bulb has a different value. ☐

The current through each bulb has the same value. ☐ **[2 marks]**

Turn over >

09 A student plans to use the apparatus in **Figure 9.1** to compare the insulation properties of different materials.

The insulating material is sandwiched between the inner beaker and the outer beaker.

Hot water is poured into the inner beaker.

The rate at which the hot water cools is a measure of the thermal insulation property of the material.

Figure 9.1

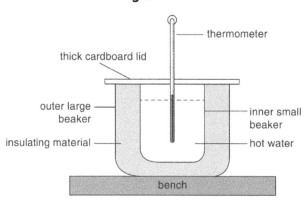

09.1 Write a set of instructions for the student, to give valid data that can be used to compare the insulation properties of different materials.

Include instructions for keeping all control variables constant.

Specify any additional apparatus that is required.

Explain how the data generated can be used to compare the insulation property of the materials tested.

....

....

....

....

....

....

....

....

[6 marks]

09.2 The insulating materials used by the student in the experiment are listed in **Table 9.1** with their thermal conductivity values.

Table 9.1

Material	Thermal conductivity in W/(m K)
Sheep's wool	0.039
Feathers	0.034
Cotton wool	0.029

Which of the materials in the table is the best thermal insulator?

[1 mark]

Question 9 continues on the next page

09.3 Figure 9.2 gives information about the conduction of thermal energy through stone walls.

Figure 9.2

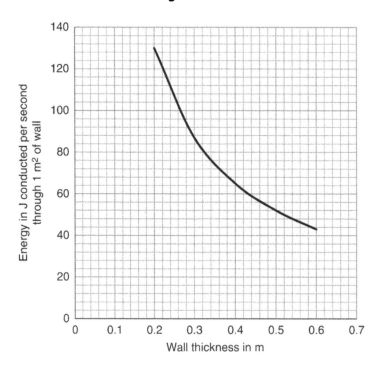

Write a conclusion about the effect of wall thickness on the energy conducted per second through 1 m² of stone wall.

Select appropriate data from **Figure 9.2** to support your conclusion.

....

....

....

....

.... **[3 marks]**

10.1 **Figure 10.1** shows a sealed copper vessel containing air.

A gauge attached to the copper vessel shows the pressure of the air inside.

Figure 10.1

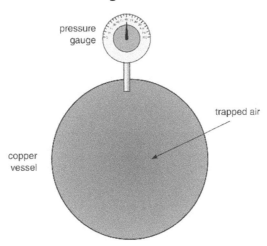

Describe the motion of the air molecules inside the copper vessel.

....

[1 mark]

10.2 Describe how the air inside the copper vessel in **Figure 10.1** exerts pressure on the inside wall of the vessel.

....

....

[1 mark]

Question 10 continues on the next page

10.3 The copper vessel in **Figure 10.1** is lowered into a hot water bath.

This raises the temperature and the pressure of the air inside.

The volume of the copper vessel does not change.

Explain why the increase in temperature affects the pressure of the air inside the vessel.

....

....

....

.... **[2 marks]**

10.4 **Figure 10.2(a)** shows a gas-filled cylinder.

It is sealed by a moveable piston.

Figure 10.2

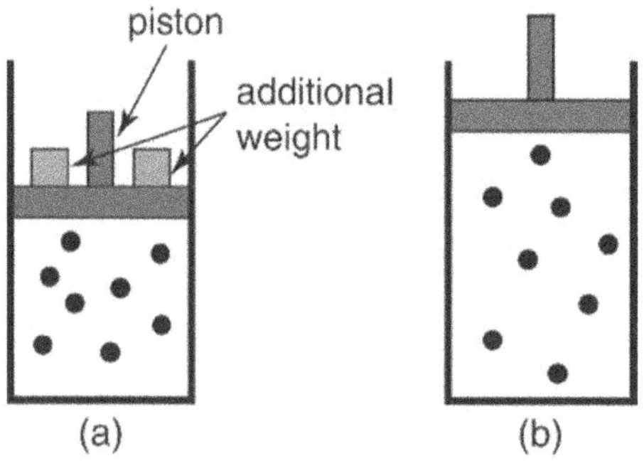

The volume of the gas is 2.4×10^{-3} m³

The gas pressure is 1.0×10^5 Pa

When the additional weights are slowly removed, the gas expands to a new volume of 3.2×10^{-3} m³ with no change in temperature **(Figure 10.2(b))**.

Calculate the new gas pressure.

....

....

....

New pressure = ... Pa   **[3 marks]**

10.5 A large downward force is now applied quickly to the piston in **Figure 10.2(b)**.

This rapidly compresses the gas inside, causing an increase in temperature.

What is the effect of the work done by the downward force?

Write **one** tick in **each** row.

Quantity	Increases	Decreases	Doesn't change
Internal energy of the molecules			
Average molecule speed			
Average separation of the molecules			

[3 marks]

Turn over >

11.1 A cyclist cycles to the top of a small hill of height 10 m

When he reaches the top of the hill, he freewheels down the other side.

As he freewheels down the hill, 50% of his gravitational potential energy is dissipated to the surroundings as thermal energy.

Calculate the speed of the cyclist as he reaches the bottom of the hill.

The mass of the cyclist and his bicycle is 100 kg

Take gravitational field strength = 10 N/kg

Speed = ... m/s   **[5 marks]**

END OF QUESTIONS

BLANK PAGE

Physics Equation Sheet

Equation Number	Word Equation	Symbol Equation
1	pressure due to a column of liquid = height of column × density of liquid × gravitational field strength	$p = h \rho g$
2	(final velocity)^2 − (initial velocity)^2 = 2 × acceleration × distance	$v^2 - u^2 = 2as$
3	force = $\dfrac{\text{change in momentum}}{\text{time taken}}$	$F = \dfrac{m\Delta v}{\Delta t}$
4	elastic potential energy = 0.5 × spring constant × (extension)^2	$E_e = \dfrac{1}{2}ke^2$
5	change in thermal energy = mass × specific heat capacity × temperature change	$\Delta E = mc\Delta\theta$
6	period = $\dfrac{1}{\text{frequency}}$	
7	magnification = $\dfrac{\text{image height}}{\text{object height}}$	
8	force on a conductor (at right-angles to a magnetic field) carrying a current = magnetic flux density × current × length	$F = BIl$
9	thermal energy for a change of state = mass × specific latent heat	$E = mL$
10	$\dfrac{\text{potential difference across primary coil}}{\text{potential difference across secondary coil}}$ = $\dfrac{\text{number of turns in primary coil}}{\text{number of turns in seconday coil}}$	$\dfrac{V_p}{V_s} = \dfrac{n_p}{n_s}$
11	potential difference across primary coil × current in primary coil = potential difference across secondary coil × current in secondary coil	$V_p I_p = V_s I_s$
12	For gases: pressure × volume = constant	$pV = \text{constant}$

Collins

AQA

GCSE

PHYSICS

SET A – Paper 2 Higher Tier

Author: Lynn Pharaoh

Time allowed: 1 hour 45 minutes

Materials

For this paper you must have:
• a ruler
• a calculator
• the Physics Equation Sheet (found at the end of the paper).

Instructions

• Answer **all** questions in the spaces provided.
• Do all rough work in this book. Cross through any work you do not want to be marked.

Information

• There are 100 marks available on this paper.
• The marks for questions are shown in brackets.
• You are expected to use a calculator where appropriate.
• You are reminded of the need for good English and clear presentation in your answers.
• When answering questions 03.1, 05.3 and 10 you need to make sure that your answer:
  – is clear, logical, sensibly structured
  – fully meets the requirements of the question
  – shows that each separate point or step supports the overall answer.

Advice

• In all calculations, show clearly how you work out your answer.

Name:

01.1 A sound wave is described as a **longitudinal wave**.

Describe **one** defining feature of a longitudinal wave.

....

.... **[1 mark]**

01.2 **Table 1.1** shows the speed at which sound travels through various materials.

Table 1.1

Material	Speed of sound in m/s
air	343
helium	972
water	1481
seawater	1522
brick	4000
steel	5000

Give **three** conclusions that can be made from the data in **Table 1.1**

1. ....

....

2. ....

....

3. .... **[3 marks]**

01.3 Write down the equation that links wave speed, frequency and wavelength.

.... **[1 mark]**

01.4 A sound wave is produced by a loudspeaker at a frequency of 500 Hz

The sound wave travels through a brick wall.

Calculate the wavelength of the sound wave while it is travelling through the wall.

Select the required data from **Table 1.1**

....

....

Wavelength = ... m **[3 marks]**

01.5 What is the frequency range of normal human hearing?

Tick **one** box.

200 Hz to 200 kHz ☐

20 Hz to 20 kHz ☐

2 Hz to 2kHz ☐   **[1 mark]**

01.6 Ultrasound waves have a frequency above the upper limit of hearing for humans.

Give an application of ultrasound waves.

.... **[1 mark]**

Turn over >

02.1 Which **two** of the following statements represent Newton's first law of motion?

Tick **two** boxes.

The resultant force on a stationary object is zero. ☐

Acceleration is proportional to resultant force. ☐

When two objects exert a force on each other, the forces are equal and opposite. ☐

The resultant force on an object moving at a steady speed is zero. ☐ **[2 marks]**

02.2 The two main resistive forces acting on a cyclist and his bicycle are:

- air resistance
- rolling resistance between the bicycle's tyres and the road.

Figure 2.1 shows how these two forces vary with the bicycle's speed.

Figure 2.1

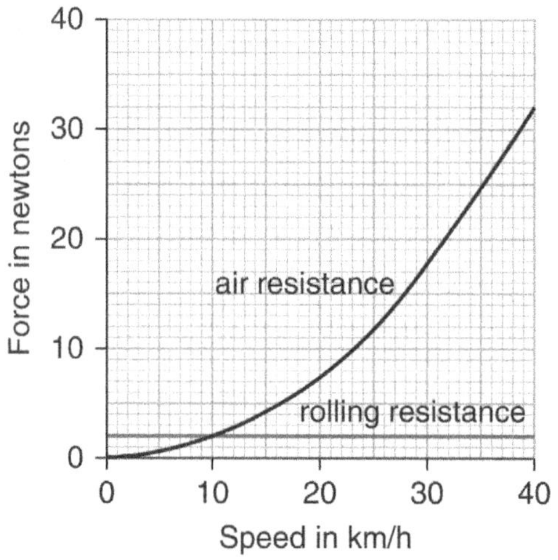

Write down **three** conclusions that you can make from **Figure 2.1**

1. ....

   ....

2. ....

   ....

3. ....

   .... **[3 marks]**

02.3 Use **Figure 2.1** to determine the **total resistive force** acting on the cyclist and his bicycle when travelling at a steady speed of 20 km/h

Total resistive force = _____ N **[3 marks]**

02.4 Write down the equation which links work done, force and distance travelled.

[1 mark]

02.5 Calculate the work done by the cyclist in maintaining a steady speed of 20 km/hour over a distance of 200 m along a flat road.

Give the correct unit with your answer.

Work done = _____

Unit: _____ **[3 marks]**

02.6 Write down the equation that links resultant force, mass and acceleration.

[1 mark]

02.7 The cyclist now pedals faster so that he accelerates at 2.0 m/s²

The mass of the cyclist and his bicycle is 70 kg

Calculate the resultant force on the cyclist and his bicycle.

Resultant force = _____ N **[2 marks]**

Turn over >

03 A student uses the apparatus in **Figure 3.1** to obtain data on the extension of a spring under a stretching force.

Figure 3.1

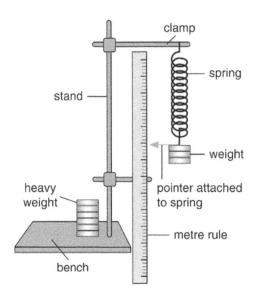

03.1 Describe how an accurate extension measurement is obtained when a specific weight is attached to the spring in **Figure 3.1**

Include a description of how errors can be kept to a minimum.

_____

_____

_____

_____

_____

_____

_____

_____

[4 marks]

03.2 **Figure 3.2** shows the student's extension and stretching force data plotted on a graph.

Figure 3.2

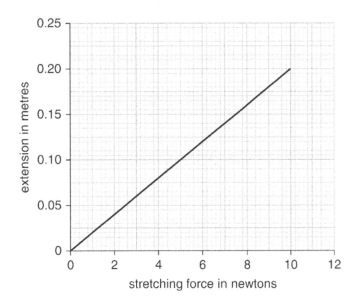

Give **two** conclusions from the graph about the behaviour of the spring.

1. ....

....

2. ....

.... **[2 marks]**

03.3 Write down the equation that links force, spring constant and extension.

.... **[1 mark]**

03.4 Calculate the spring constant of the spring.

Use data from **Figure 3.2**

....

....

....

Spring constant = ... N/m **[4 marks]**

Turn over >

04.1 **Figure 4.1** is a plan view of a gate.

Figure 4.1

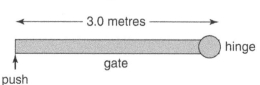

A moment of 18 N m is needed to open the gate.

The gate is pushed where shown in **Figure 4.1**

Calculate the push force that must be applied to open the gate.

Force = _____ N **[2 marks]**

04.2 A gardener is applying an upward force to the handle of the wheelbarrow as shown in **Figure 4.2**

The wheelbarrow is stationary and is balanced with its back legs just off the ground.

Figure 4.2

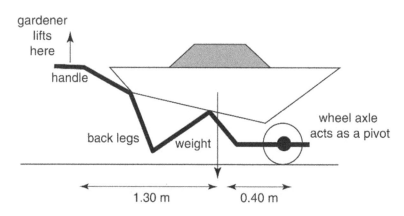

The total weight of the wheelbarrow and its contents is 400 N

Calculate the upward force exerted by the gardener on the handle of the wheelbarrow.

Give your answer to two significant figures.

Force = _____ N **[3 marks]**

05.1 A car is travelling down a test track as part of a crash safety test.

The car has a velocity of 10 m/s

A crash dummy in the driver's seat of the car has a mass of 60 kg

Calculate the crash dummy's momentum.

Momentum = _____ kg m/s   **[1 mark]**

05.2 As part of the safety test, the car crashes into a barrier.

The crash dummy has no seat belt or air bag. It hits the windscreen and comes to a stop in 0.1 s

Calculate the impact force on the crash dummy.

Select the correct equation from the Physics Equation Sheet.

Force = _____ N   **[2 marks]**

05.3 An air bag is now fitted to the car for driver protection.

Explain the effect that the air bag will have on the crash dummy in a similar test crash.

[4 marks]

Turn over >

06.1 **Figure 6.1** shows a tall can with three holes at different heights.

The can is continuously filled with water, which spurts out through the three holes.

Figure 6.1

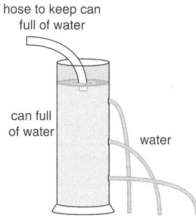

Explain why the three jets of water from the three holes take the shapes shown.

....

....

.... **[2 marks]**

06.2 Calculate the water pressure at a depth of 1.0 km below the surface of the sea.

Gravitational field strength = 9.8 N/kg

Density of seawater = 1030 kg/m³

Select the correct equation from the Physics Equation Sheet.

Give your answer in standard form to 2 significant figures.

....

....

Water pressure = ... Pa **[3 marks]**

06.3 **Figure 6.2** shows how atmospheric pressure changes with height above sea level.

Figure 6.2

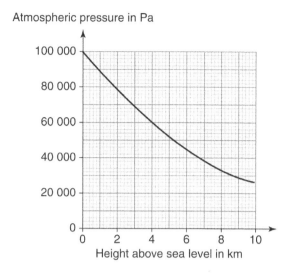

Describe the relationship shown by the graph.

_____

_____

[1 mark]

06.4 A student suggests that the graph in **Figure 6.2** shows that atmospheric pressure **halves** when height above sea level **doubles**.

Is the student's suggestion correct?

Justify your answer using data from the graph.

_____

_____

_____

_____

_____

[3 marks]

Turn over >

07 A student investigates the refraction of light at the boundary between air and a transparent solid block.

She directs a ray of light from a ray box at a specific angle of incidence at the block (**Figure 7.1**).

She marks the path of the ray through the block.

She measures the angle of refraction produced for the following angles of incidence:

20°, 30°, 40°, 50°, 60°, 70°

07.1 Identify the independent, dependent and control variables in this investigation.

Independent variable: ....

Dependent variable: ....

Control variable: ....   **[3 marks]**

07.2 Complete the path of the ray in **Figure 7.1**:

- as it is refracted within the transparent block
- as it emerges from the block.

Figure 7.1

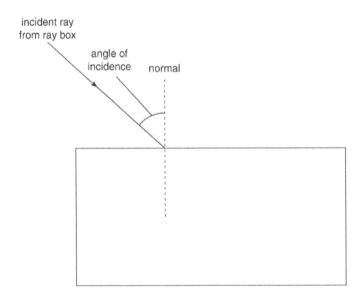

[2 marks]

07.3 **Table 7.1** shows the student's measurements.

Table 7.1

Angle of incidence in degrees	20	30	40	50	60	70	80
Angle of refraction in degrees	13	20	26	31	36	39	41

Figure 7.2 is a graph of the student's data, but it is incomplete.

Plot the missing points on **Figure 7.2**.

Draw a curve of best fit.

Figure 7.2

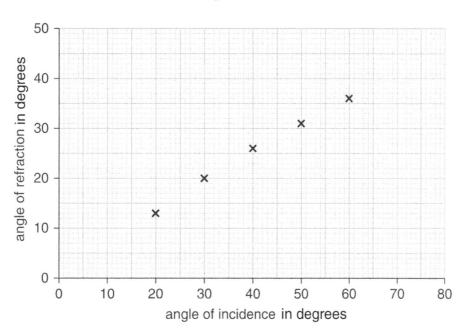

angle of incidence in degrees

[2 marks]

07.4 Give **two** conclusions based on the graph.

....

....

....

.... **[2 marks]**

Question 7 continues on the next page

07.5 **Figure 7.3** shows the light incident on the transparent block.

The incident wavefronts have been drawn.

Figure 7.3

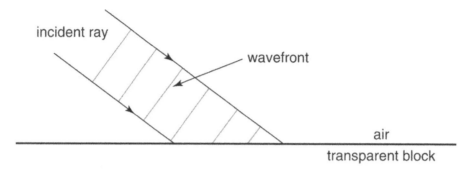

Complete the diagram by drawing **four** refracted wavefronts.   **[3 marks]**

07.6 The separation of wavefronts represents the wavelength of the light.

Describe how the wavelength of the light is affected by refraction in the transparent block.

_____   **[1 mark]**

07.7 The frequency of light is **not** affected when the light enters a different material.

Predict how the **speed** of the light is affected when it enters the transparent block from air.

Justify your prediction.

_____

_____   **[2 marks]**

08.1 Figure 8.1 shows bar magnet and a copper coil wrapped around a cardboard tube.

Figure 8.1

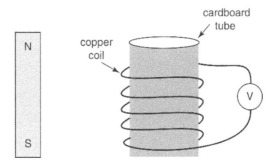

A student wants to induce a potential difference across the copper coil.

He can move either the magnet or the coil.

Describe **two** actions that he could carry out to produce a reading on the voltmeter.

....

....

....

.... **[2 marks]**

Question 8 continues on the next page

08.2 **Figure 8.2** represents a hand-driven a.c. generator.

Figure 8.2

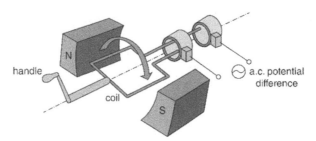

Explain why the generator in **Figure 8.2** produces a potential difference while the handle is being rotated.

....

....

.... **[2 marks]**

08.3 **Figure 8.3** shows the output potential difference from the a.c. generator as the handle is rotated.

Figure 8.3

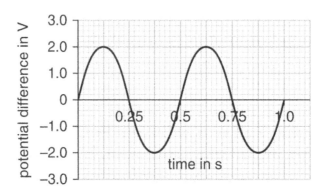

What feature of the graph shows that the output of the generator is a.c.?

....

.... **[1 mark]**

08.4 Use **Figure 8.3** to determine the time for the handle of the generator to complete one revolution.

Time = _____ s   **[1 mark]**

08.5 Use **Figure 8.3** to determine the generator's maximum output potential difference.

Potential difference = _____ V   **[1 mark]**

08.6 State **two** ways in which the graph in **Figure 8.3** would change if the handle were rotated at a faster speed.

_____

_____

_____

_____ **[2 marks]**

Turn over >

09   **Figure 9.1** shows the magnetic field between two magnets.

The faces of the magnets are the poles and they are positioned with opposite poles facing.

Figure 9.1

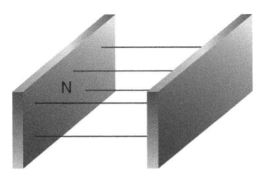

09.1 Add arrows to the field lines in **Figure 9.1** to show the direction of the magnetic field between the magnets.

[1 mark]

09.2 A wire carrying an electric current is placed between the poles of the two magnets (**Figure 9.2**).

Figure 9.2

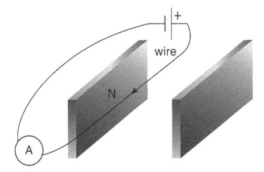

The arrow on the wire shows the direction of the current.

Use Fleming's left-hand rule to determine the direction of the force on the wire.

Draw an arrow on **Figure 9.2** to show the direction of the force on the wire.

[1 mark]

09.3 The current in the wire in **Figure 9.2** is 3.2 A

The magnetic flux density of the magnetic field is 0.20 T

The length of wire within the field is 5.0 cm

Select the correct equation from the Physics Equation Sheet to calculate the size of the force on the wire.

_____

_____

Force = _____ N **[2 marks]**

09.4 **Figure 9.3** is a diagram of a d.c. electric motor.

Figure 9.3

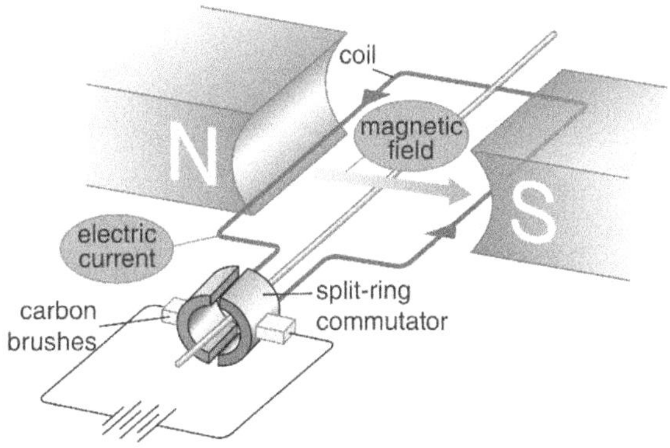

Explain why the coil of the motor rotates.

_____

_____

_____

[3 marks]

10.1 The life cycle of a star is determined by the mass of the star.

Describe the life cycles of **both**:

- a star the size of the Sun, and
- a star which is much more massive.

Outline their similarities and differences.

[6 marks]

11.1 A car is driven along a straight road.

Figure 11.1 shows the car's velocity–time graph during the first 20 s of its motion.

Figure 11.1

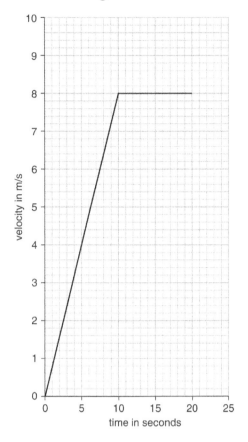

velocity in m/s

time in seconds

Determine the car's acceleration during the **first 10 s** of its motion.

Acceleration = _____ m/s² **[2 marks]**

Question 11 continues on the next page

11.2 **Use Figure 11.1** to determine the **average speed of** the car during the first **20 s** of motion.

Show your working.

Average speed = _____ m/s **[4 marks]**

END OF QUESTIONS

BLANK PAGE

Physics Equation Sheet

Equation Number	Word Equation	Symbol Equation
1	pressure due to a column of liquid = height of column × density of liquid × gravitational field strength	$p = h \rho g$
2	(final velocity)² – (initial velocity)² = 2 × acceleration × distance	$v^2 - u^2 = 2\,a\,s$
3	force = $\dfrac{\text{change in momentum}}{\text{time taken}}$	$F = \dfrac{m\Delta v}{\Delta t}$
4	elastic potential energy = 0.5 × spring constant × (extension)²	$E_e = \dfrac{1}{2}\,ke^2$
5	change in thermal energy = mass × specific heat capacity × temperature change	$\Delta E = m\,c\,\Delta\theta$
6	period = $\dfrac{1}{\text{frequency}}$	
7	magnification = $\dfrac{\text{image height}}{\text{object height}}$	
8	force on a conductor (at right-angles to a magnetic field) carrying a current = magnetic flux density × current × length	$F = B\,I\,l$
9	thermal energy for a change of state = mass × specific latent heat	$E = m\,L$
10	$\dfrac{\text{potential difference across primary coil}}{\text{potential difference across secondary coil}}$ = $\dfrac{\text{number of turns in primary coil}}{\text{number of turns in seconday coil}}$	$\dfrac{V_p}{V_s} = \dfrac{n_p}{n_s}$
11	potential difference across primary coil × current in primary coil = potential difference across secondary coil × current in secondary coil	$V_p I_p = V_s I_s$
12	For gases: pressure × volume = constant	$pV = \text{constant}$

Collins

AQA
GCSE
PHYSICS
SET B – Paper 1 Higher Tier

Author: Lynn Pharaoh

H

Time allowed: 1 hour 45 minutes

Materials

For this paper you must have:

- a ruler
- a calculator
- the Physics Equation Sheet (found at the end of the paper).

Instructions

- Answer **all** questions in the spaces provided.
- Do all rough work in this book. Cross through any work you do not want to be marked.

Information

- There are 100 marks available on this paper.
- The marks for questions are shown in brackets.
- You are expected to use a calculator where appropriate.
- You are reminded of the need for good English and clear presentation in your answers.
- When answering questions 01.1, 02.1 and 08.1 you need to make sure that your answer:
  - is clear, logical, sensibly structured
  - fully meets the requirements of the question
  - shows that each separate point or step supports the overall answer.

Advice

- In all calculations, show clearly how you work out your answer.

Name: _____

01.1 Compare the motion and arrangement of particles when a substance is in its **solid** state, **liquid** state and **gas** state.

....

....

....

....

....

....

....

.... **[4 marks]**

01.2 What is meant by the **internal energy** of a material?

....

....

.... **[3 marks]**

01.3 Which **two** of the changes below would cause an **increase** in the internal energy of a volume of liquid water?

Tick **two** boxes.

The water temperature is increased ☐

The water is changed to ice at 0°C ☐

The water is changed to steam at 100°C ☐

The water temperature is decreased ☐ **[2 marks]**

02.1 A student wants to demonstrate to her class that:

Two objects that carry the same type of charge repel

Two objects that carry different types of charge attract

The apparatus the student has is:

1. a piece of cloth

2. two acetate rods

3. two polythene rods

4. a way to suspend a rod so that it can move freely, as shown in **Figure 2.1**

Figure 2.1

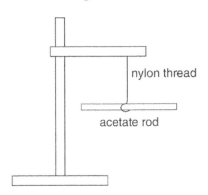

Describe the demonstration that the student should do for the class.

Use this information:

• polythene can gain a negative charge

• acetate can gain a positive charge.

_____

_____

_____

_____

_____

_____

_____

[4 marks]

Question 2 continues on the next page

02.2 A polythene rod is used to give a negative charge to the surface of a small metal sphere shown in **Figure 2.2**

Figure 2.2

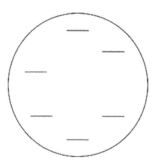

Draw **at least four** electric field lines on **Figure 2.2** to show the pattern of the electric field created by the charge on the sphere.

[2 marks]

02.3 The student gives another sphere a negative charge.

She moves the second sphere towards the first.

Which is the correct description of the force between the two charged spheres as they are moved closer together?

Tick **one** box.

An attractive force getting bigger ☐

A repulsive force getting bigger ☐

An attractive force getting smaller ☐

A repulsive force getting smaller ☐

[1 mark]

03 **Figure 3.1** shows a circuit diagram containing components X and Y.

Figure 3.1

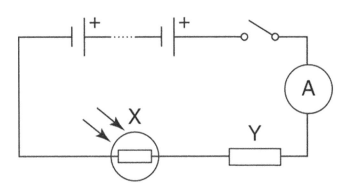

03.1 Give the name of component X.

_____ **[1 mark]**

03.2 In daylight, X has a resistance of 40 Ω

Y has a resistance of 460 Ω

Determine the total resistance in the circuit.

Total resistance = _____ Ω **[1 mark]**

03.3 Write down the equation linking potential difference, current and resistance.

_____ **[1 mark]**

Question 3 continues on the next page

03.4 The battery supplies a potential difference of 12 V to the circuit.

Calculate the expected reading on the ammeter during daylight when the switch is closed.

_____

_____

Ammeter reading = _____ A   **[3 marks]**

03.5 **Figure 3.2** is a sketch graph showing how the resistance of component X varies as the brightness of the light shining on it changes.

Figure 3.2

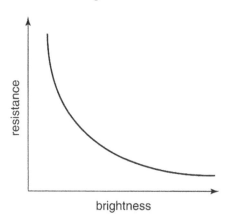

Use **Figure 3.2** to predict how the ammeter reading would change if the circuit was in darkness when the switch was closed.

Explain your answer.

_____

_____

_____ **[2 marks]**

04.1 A student wants to find out if a length of wire behaves as an ohmic conductor.

She needs a circuit to measure the current through the wire for various values of potential difference across the wire.

She has crocodile clips, X and Y, to connect to the ends of the wire.

Complete the circuit diagram in **Figure 4.1** to enable her to take the measurements.

Figure 4.1

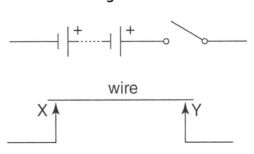

[3 marks]

Question 4 continues on the next page

04.2 **Figure 4.2** is a sketch graph of the student's current and potential difference data for the wire.

Figure 4.2

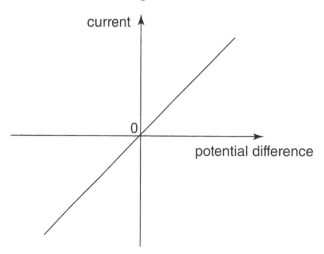

What can be concluded from **Figure 4.2** about the relationship between current and potential difference?

Is the wire an ohmic conductor?

....

....

.... **[2 marks]**

 ©HarperCollins*Publishers* 2019

04.3 The student replaced the wire between the crocodile clips with a filament bulb.

Sketch the graph of current against potential difference that the student would expect for the filament bulb.

Use the axes in **Figure 4.3**

Figure 4.3

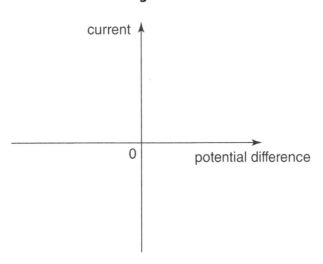

[2 marks]

04.4 Explain why the resistance of a filament bulb changes as the current through it is increased.

....

....

....

.... [2 marks]

05.1 A radioactive tracer is put into a patient's body to investigate an organ that may not be functioning normally.

A detector is used to detect the radiation emitted by the tracer atoms.

Explain why a radioactive isotope that emits alpha radiation is **not** suitable for use as a tracer.

....

....

....

.... **[2 marks]**

05.2 The most commonly used medical tracer is technetium-99

Technetium-99 has a half-life of 6 hours.

Explain why a half-life of 6 hours makes technetium-99 suitable for use as a tracer.

....

....

....

.... **[2 marks]**

05.3 The radioactive isotope iodine-131 is used to destroy cancerous cells in the thyroid gland.

The radioactive iodine is given to the patient in the form of a capsule which they eat.

Iodine-131 emits beta and gamma radiation.

It has a half-life of 8 days.

Explain why the patient would have to spend time in hospital isolated from other people.

....

....

....

.... **[3 marks]**

06 A student is experimenting with a child's loop-the-loop track for toy cars, as shown in **Figure 6.1**

Figure 6.1

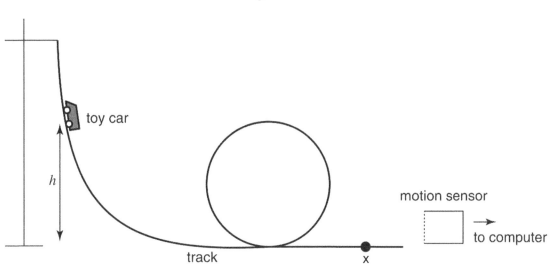

The student gradually increases the height (*h*) from which the toy car is released.

Eventually, the car has enough energy to complete the loop and travel along the track towards the motion sensor.

The motion sensor and computer record the speed of the car as it passes point X.

06.1 The student finds that if the car is released at a height of *h* = 42 cm, it stays on the track and reaches the motion sensor.

Calculate the gain in the car's gravitational potential energy store by lifting it to height *h* = 42 cm

The mass of the toy car is 0.050 kg

Take gravitational field strength = 10 N/kg

Gain in gravitational potential energy = ... J **[2 marks]**

Question 6 continues on the next page

06.2 At point X in **Figure 6.1**, the motion sensor records the car's speed as 2.0 m/s

Calculate the car's kinetic energy.

_____

_____

Kinetic energy = _____ J **[2 marks]**

06.3 Give a reason why the kinetic energy value at **X** must be less than the gravitational potential energy value at height $h = 0.42$ cm

_____

_____ **[1 mark]**

07 A temperature sensor inside an electric kettle measures the water temperature every 5.0 s as the water is heated.

Figure 7.1 shows the graph of the temperature data that was recorded.

Figure 7.1

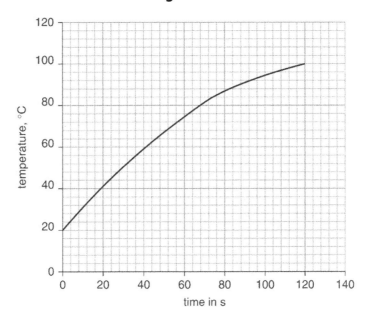

07.1 Determine the gradient of the line in **Figure 7.1** at 80 s

Show on the graph how you obtained your answer.

....

....

....

Gradient = ...°C/s **[2 marks]**

Question 7 continues on the next page

07.2 The gradient of the line in **Figure 7.1** represents the water's **temperature rise per second**.

What can be concluded about how the water's temperature rise per second changes as the water gets hotter?

Use data from the graph to support your answer.

....

....

....

.... **[2 marks]**

07.3 What can be concluded about the **rate of dissipation** of thermal energy to the surroundings as the water temperature rises?

....

.... **[1 mark]**

07.4 **Table 7.1** shows the thermal conductivity of materials used for the outer casing of different kettles.

Table 7.1

Material	Thermal conductivity in W/(m K)
Steel	16
polyethylene	0.33
polypropylene	0.22

It is desirable to minimise the rate of energy transfer from the water through the outer casing of the kettle.

Which material from **Table 7.1** is most suitable?

Explain your answer.

....

....

.... **[2 marks]**

08.1 Figure 8.1 shows apparatus that can be used to measure the volume of a pebble, in order to determine the pebble's density.

The measuring cylinder measures up to 50 cm³ and has 1 cm³ graduations.

Figure 8.1

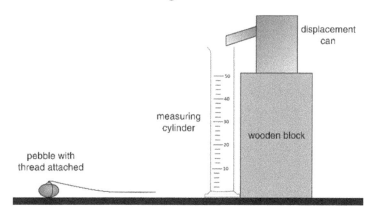

Write a series of instructions to determine the volume and density of the pebble.

State any additional laboratory apparatus that may be required.

Suggest how errors can be kept as small as possible.

[6 marks]

Question 8 continues on the next page

08.2 A student suggests an alternative method to determine the volume of the **same** pebble.

He suggests lowering the pebble into a much larger measuring cylinder which already contains water **(Figure 8.2)**.

Figure 8.2

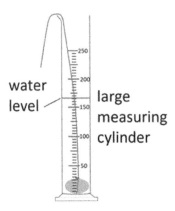

Describe how this apparatus can be used to determine the **volume** of the pebble.

....

....

....

....

.... **[3 marks]**

08.3 Using the method in **Figure 8.2,** the student chooses a measuring cylinder that measures up to 250 cm³ and has 5 cm³ graduations.

Compare the accuracy of the volume measurement using this method with the accuracy using the method shown in **Figure 8.1**

....

....

....

.... **[2 marks]**

09.1 When a uranium nucleus undergoes fission, it splits into two daughter nuclei called **fission fragments**.

Typically, two to three free neutrons are also released.

Describe what must happen for a chain reaction to become established in a sample of uranium.

_____

_____

_____

_____

[3 marks]

09.2 When a chain reaction occurs in uranium, the mass numbers of the fission fragments produced vary between 70 and 170

The graph in **Figure 9.1** shows the typical distribution of the fission fragment mass numbers for the fission of uranium.

Figure 9.1

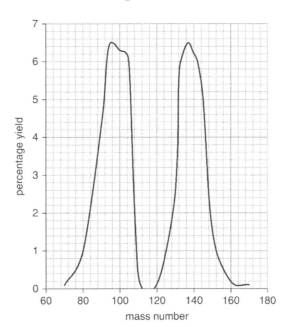

Determine the **two most probable** mass numbers of the fission fragments produced in the fission of uranium.

Use the data shown in **Figure 9.1**

_____

[2 marks]

Question 9 continues on the next page

09.3 Fission fragment nuclei are unstable.

One example of a fission fragment is strontium, $^{90}_{38}$Sr

Give the numbers of the different subatomic particles present in a strontium nucleus.

....

.... **[2 marks]**

09.4 Strontium-90 decays by beta emission to form an isotope of yttrium.

Complete the decay equation for strontium-90

$$^{90}_{38}\text{Sr} \longrightarrow \quad \text{Y} + \quad \text{e}$$

[2 marks]

09.5 Strontium-90 has a half-life of 30 years.

What fraction of a sample of strontium-90 remains after 120 years have passed?

....

Fraction = ... **[1 mark]**

09.6 The uranium fuel used at a nuclear power station is an alpha emitter.

The fission fragments produced in the power station are mostly beta emitters.

Explain why the fission fragments create a greater hazard to the workers at the power station than the uranium fuel.

....

.... **[2 marks]**

09.7 Material containing fission fragments forms some of the nuclear waste produced by a nuclear power station.

Table 9.1 lists some of the fission fragment isotopes, and gives their half-life values.

Table 9.1

Fission fragment	Half-life
Barium-140	12 days
Caesium-137	30 years
Caesium-139	9 minutes
Iodine-131	8 days
Krypton-85	11 years
Xenon-140	14 s

Name **two** fission fragments from **Table 9.1** that will require long-term safe storage.

....

.... [2 marks]

Turn over >

10.1 A change of state of a substance is described as a physical change.

Explain what is meant by a **physical change**.

....

.... **[1 mark]**

10.2 **Figure 10.1** shows the heating graph for a substance being heated at a constant rate.

Figure 10.1

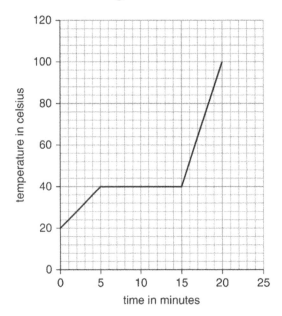

Determine the melting point of the substance.

Melting point = ... °C   **[1 mark]**

10.3 Use **Figure 10.1** to determine the time taken for the substance to change entirely from its solid state to its liquid state.

Time = _____ minutes   **[1 mark]**

10.4 The power of the electrical heater used to heat the substance was 50 W

The substance had a mass of 0.10 kg

Calculate the specific latent heat of fusion of the substance.

_____

_____

_____

_____

Specific latent heat of fusion = _____ J/kg **[5 marks]**

10.5 Look again at the graph in **Figure 10.1**

Determine whether the **specific heat capacity** of the substance in its solid state is **larger** or **smaller** than its specific heat capacity in its liquid state.

Explain your answer.

_____

_____

_____

[2 marks]

Turn over >

11   A student uses the apparatus in the circuit shown in **Figure 11.1** to measure the specific heat capacity of a metal block.

Figure 11.1

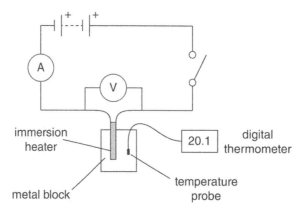

11.1 The battery supplies approximately 9 V of potential difference.

The resistance of the immersion heater is approximately 15 Ω

Calculate an approximate value for the current drawn from the battery by the immersion heater.

Current ≈ _____ A   **[3 marks]**

11.2 The student has three different ammeters to choose from for the experiment.

Details of the three ammeters, X, Y and Z, are shown in **Table 11.1**

Table 11.1

Ammeter	Maximum current reading, in A	Value of the smallest division, in A
X	2	0.1
Y	1	0.05
Z	0.5	0.02

Which would be the most suitable ammeter to measure the current in the circuit?

Explain your answer.

[3 marks]

11.3 The student closes the switch in the circuit (**Figure 11.1**).

The heater raises the temperature of the metal block.

The student's measurements are shown in **Table 11.2**

Table 11.2

Quantity	Measurement
Mass of block	0.50 kg
Initial temperature	20.1°C
Final temperature	30.1 °C
Current	0.55 A
Potential difference	8.0 V
Heating time	500 s

Use the student's measurements to calculate the energy supplied by the heater.

Energy supplied = _____ J **[3 marks]**

11.4 Use your answer to question 11.3 and the student's data in **Table 11.2** to calculate the specific heat capacity of the metal block.

Give the correct unit with your answer.

Specific heat capacity = _____

Unit: _____ **[4 marks]**

END OF QUESTIONS

Physics Equation Sheet

Equation Number	Word Equation	Symbol Equation
1	pressure due to a column of liquid = height of column × density of liquid × gravitational field strength	$p = h \rho g$
2	(final velocity)² – (initial velocity)² = 2 × acceleration × distance	$v^2 - u^2 = 2\,a\,s$
3	force = $\dfrac{\text{change in momentum}}{\text{time taken}}$	$F = \dfrac{m\Delta v}{\Delta t}$
4	elastic potential energy = 0.5 × spring constant × (extension)²	$E_e = \dfrac{1}{2}\,ke^2$
5	change in thermal energy = mass × specific heat capacity × temperature change	$\Delta E = m\,c\,\Delta\theta$
6	period = $\dfrac{1}{\text{frequency}}$	
7	magnification = $\dfrac{\text{image height}}{\text{object height}}$	
8	force on a conductor (at right-angles to a magnetic field) carrying a current = magnetic flux density × current × length	$F = B\,I\,l$
9	thermal energy for a change of state = mass × specific latent heat	$E = m\,L$
10	$\dfrac{\text{potential difference across primary coil}}{\text{potential difference across secondary coil}}$ = $\dfrac{\text{number of turns in primary coil}}{\text{number of turns in seconday coil}}$	$\dfrac{V_p}{V_s} = \dfrac{n_p}{n_s}$
11	potential difference across primary coil × current in primary coil = potential difference across secondary coil × current in secondary coil	$V_p I_p = V_s I_s$
12	For gases: pressure × volume = constant	$pV = \text{constant}$

Collins

AQA

GCSE

PHYSICS

H

SET B – Paper 2 Higher Tier

Author: Lynn Pharaoh

Time allowed: 1 hour 45 minutes

Materials

For this paper you must have:

- a ruler
- a calculator
- the Physics Equation Sheet (found at the end of the paper).

Instructions

- Answer **all** questions in the spaces provided.
- Do all rough work in this book. Cross through any work you do not want to be marked.

Information

- There are 100 marks available on this paper.
- The marks for questions are shown in brackets.
- You are expected to use a calculator where appropriate.
- You are reminded of the need for good English and clear presentation in your answers.
- When answering questions 06.2, 09.1 and 11.1 you need to make sure that your answer:
  - is clear, logical, sensibly structured
  - fully meets the requirements of the question
  - shows that each separate point or step supports the overall answer.

Advice

- In all calculations, show clearly how you work out your answer.

Name: _____

01.1 **Figure 1.1** shows the path of a ray of light through a convex lens.

Figure 1.1

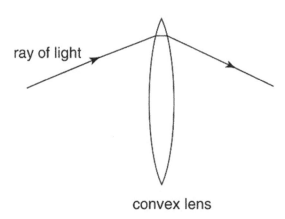

convex lens

What is the name given to the bending of light at the boundaries between the lens and air?

.... **[1 mark]**

01.2 Complete the ray diagram in **Figure 1.2** to show the formation of an image of the object (O) by the convex lens.

Label the image formed.

Figure 1.2

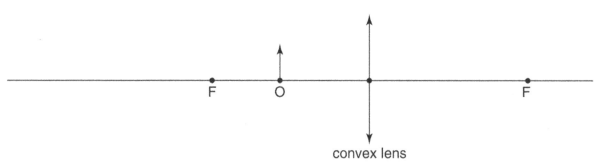

convex lens

[4 marks]

01.3 Which **two** descriptions of the images formed by a convex lens are correct?

Tick **two** boxes.

Always real ☐

Always virtual ☐

Can be either real or virtual ☐

Always upright ☐

Always upside down ☐

Can be either upright or upside down ☐ **[2 marks]**

01.4 Which **two** descriptions of the images formed by a **concave** lens are correct?

Tick **two** boxes.

Always real ☐

Always virtual ☐

Can be either real or virtual ☐

Always upright ☐

Always upside down ☐

Can be either upright or upside down ☐ **[2 marks]**

Turn over >

02   **Figure 2.1** shows a high diving board at a swimming pool.

A ball is stationary on the diving board.

Figure 2.1

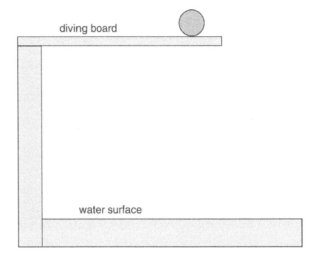

02.1 Identify the **two** forces acting on the ball in **Figure 2.1**

1. _____

2. _____   **[2 marks]**

02.2 The ball is pushed gently so that it falls over the end of the diving board.

When the ball hits the water surface, it floats and is stationary.

Figure 2.2 is a sketch of a velocity–time graph of the ball's motion, showing three stages in the ball's motion: A, B and C.

Figure 2.2

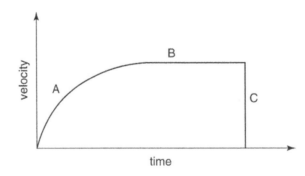

During which stage in **Figure 2.2** is there an **upward** resultant force on the ball?

Tick **one** box.

A ☐

B ☐

C ☐   **[1 mark]**

02.3 During which stage in **Figure 2.2** is there **no** resultant force on the ball?

Tick **one** box.

A ☐

B ☐

C ☐

[1 mark]

02.4 In the space below, draw a free-body force diagram of the ball during stage A
of **Figure 2.2**

Label the forces acting.

[3 marks]

02.5 Identify the **two** forces acting on the ball when it is floating on the water surface.

1. ....

2. ....

[2 marks]

03.1 The Earth completes one orbit of the Sun in 3.15×10^7 s

The distance travelled by the Earth in one orbit around the Sun is 9.42×10^{11} m

Calculate the speed of the Earth in its orbit around the Sun.

Give your answer in standard form to three significant figures.

Speed = ... m/s   **[3 marks]**

03.2 The Sun is in orbit around the centre of the Milky Way galaxy.

The mass of the Sun, to the nearest order of magnitude, is 10^{30} kg

The mass of the Milky Way galaxy, to the nearest order of magnitude, is 10^{42} kg

How many times more massive than the Sun is the Milky Way galaxy?

Give your answer as an order of magnitude.

Number of times more massive = ...   **[2 marks]**

03.3 The Sun is currently about half way through its lifetime as a main sequence star.

In about 5 billion years, the Sun will enter the next stage of its life cycle.

Name this next stage.

Suggest how this change could impact on the Earth.

....   **[2 marks]**

04.1 Astrophysicists observe **red-shift** in the light from distant galaxies.

Explain what **red-shift** means.

....

[2 marks]

04.2 Measurements of red-shift have enabled scientists to deduce that distant galaxies are moving away from the Earth.

They were able to calculate the speed at which the galaxies are receding (moving away).

Figure 4.1 is a sketch graph showing how the recession speed of galaxies varies with their distance measured from the Earth.

Figure 4.1

Explain how the observations summarised in **Figure 4.1** changed scientists' model of the universe.

....

....

....

....

[3 marks]

Turn over >

05   **Figure 5.1** shows the groups of waves in the electromagnetic spectrum.

Figure 5.1

Gamma waves	X-rays	Ultraviolet	Visible light	Infrared	Microwaves	Radio waves

05.1 Which group of waves in the electromagnetic spectrum has the **longest wavelength**?

.... **[1 mark]**

05.2 Which group of waves in the electromagnetic spectrum can be **detected with the human eye**?

.... **[1 mark]**

05.3 Which group of waves in the electromagnetic spectrum **causes skin to age prematurely**?

.... **[1 mark]**

05.4 Which **two** groups of waves in the electromagnetic spectrum can be used to cook food?

.... **[2 marks]**

05.5 An X-ray image showing a broken bone is produced by directing a beam of X-rays at the injured part of the body.

The X-rays that pass through the body are detected electronically to form an image.

Explain why X-rays are suitable for investigating a possible broken bone.

....

.... **[2 marks]**

05.6 X-rays used for medical imaging have a wavelength of 2.0×10^{-10} m

Electromagnetic waves travel at a speed of 3.0×10^8 m/s in air.

Calculate the frequency of these X-rays.

Give a suitable unit with your answer

....

....

Frequency = ...

Unit: .... **[3 marks]**

05.7 Satellites used for TV broadcasting orbit the Earth at a height well above the Earth's atmosphere.

Communication between the Earth and the satellite uses microwaves with a wavelength of about 0.1 m

Figure 5.2 provides information about the absorption of electromagnetic radiation by the Earth's atmosphere.

Figure 5.2

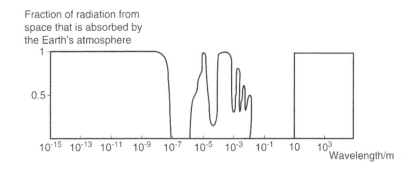

Use **Figure 5.2** to explain why microwaves of wavelength 0.1 m, rather than radio waves of typical wavelength 100 m, are used for satellite TV.

....

....

.... **[2 marks]**

Turn over >

06.1 **Figure 6.1** shows how the infrared energy radiated per second from a particular surface depends on the surface temperature.

Figure 6.1

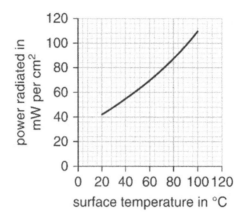

Give **two** conclusions based on the data shown in **Figure 6.1**

....

....

....

.... **[2 marks]**

06.2 A student uses the apparatus in **Figure 6.2** to investigate rate of emission of infrared radiation from different surfaces.

Figure 6.2

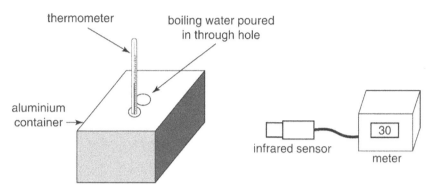

Boiling water poured into the aluminium container raises its temperature.

The infrared radiation from the container's surface is measured by the infrared sensor and displayed on the meter.

The four vertical faces of the container have a different type of surface:

- polished aluminium
- dull aluminium
- shiny black
- dull black

Write a set of instructions for the student so that the amount of infrared radiated from each of the four surfaces can be compared fairly.

Identify any variables that must be controlled.

[4 marks]

Question 6 continues on the next page

06.3 **Table 6.1** shows data generated by the experiment in **Figure 6.2**

Table 6.1

Surface	Polished aluminium	Dull aluminium	Shiny black	Dull black
Energy radiated in mW/cm²	3	23	30	33

Give **two** conclusions from the data shown in **Table 6.1**

....

....

....

.... **[2 marks]**

06.4 The wavelength of the infrared radiation emitted from a different hot object is analysed.

Figure 6.3 is a sketch graph of the results.

Figure 6.3

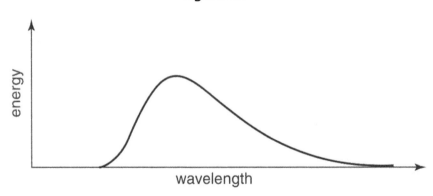

Give **two** conclusions based on **Figure 6.3**

[2 marks]

....

....

....

....

07.1 Give two **scalar** quantities.

....

[2 marks]

07.2 The distances travelled by a cyclist during the first 5.0 seconds of a road race are monitored electronically.

Figure 7.1 shows the cyclist's distance–time graph for this first 5.0 s

Figure 7.1

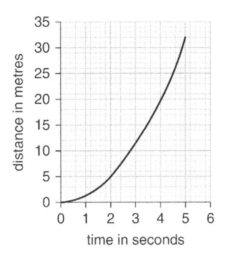

What can be concluded from **Figure 7.1** about the cyclist's motion during the first 5.0 s of the race?

Give a reason for your answer.

....

....

[2 marks]

Question 7 continues on the next page

07.3 Use **Figure 7.1** to determine the cyclist's speed 3.0 s after the start of the race.

Show your working.

....

Speed = ... m/s **[2 marks]**

07.4 Calculate the cyclist's average speed during the first 5.0 s of the race.

Use data from **Figure 7.1**

....

....

Average speed = ... m/s **[2 marks]**

08.1 A van accidentally collides with a stationary car.

Explain how the idea of the **conservation of momentum** applies to this event.

....

....

....
[2 marks]

08.2 The van has a mass of 1000 kg

Before the collision, it was moving at a velocity of 5.0 m/s

Immediately after the collision, the car moves forwards with a velocity of 4.0 m/s

The mass of the car is 800 kg

Determine the **velocity of the van** immediately after the collision.

Include its direction.

....

....

....

Van's velocity immediately after collision = ... m/s

Van's direction immediately after the collision = ... [3 marks]

Turn over >

09.1 Step-down transformers are used in laptop battery chargers and have many other uses.

Figure 9.1 shows the basic design of a step-down transformer.

Figure 9.1

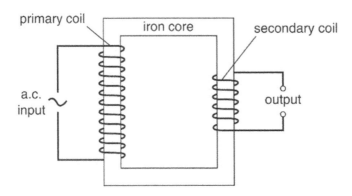

Describe the purpose of a step-down transformer.

Explain how the transformer works.

....

....

....

....

....

....

....

.... **[4 marks]**

09.2 A laptop battery charger is plugged into the mains electricity supply.

Mains electricity supplies a potential difference of 230 V

The output from the battery charger is 12 V

There are 400 turns in the primary coil of the transformer inside the battery charger.

Calculate the number of turns in the transformer's secondary coil.

Select the correct equation from the Physics Equation Sheet.

Give your answer to the nearest whole number.

Number of turns in secondary coil = ... **[3 marks]**

09.3 The current in the primary coil of the transformer in the battery charger is 0.20 A

Calculate the current in the transformer's secondary coil.

Select the correct equation from the Physics Equation Sheet.

Give your answer to 2 significant figures.

Secondary current = ... A **[3 marks]**

Turn over >

10   Newton's Second Law states that "acceleration is directly proportional to resultant force".

A student uses the air track and glider shown in **Figure 10.1** to demonstrate Newton's Second Law.

Figure 10.1

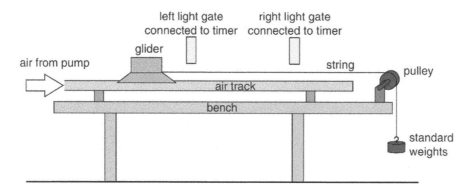

10.1 Air is pumped into the air track, lifting the glider up from the track slightly.

The glider is pulled along by the weights attached to it by string.

The times registered by the light gates enable the student to determine the acceleration of the glider.

The student plans to determine the acceleration of the glider for different weights attached to the string.

Identify the independent, dependent and control variables.

Independent variable: ....

Dependent variable: ....

Control variable: ....   **[3 marks]**

10.2 One set of the student's measurements is shown in **Table 10.1**

Table 10.1

Attached weight in N	Length of glider passing through light gate in m	Distance between light gates in m	Time to pass through first light gate in s	Time to pass through second light gate in s
0.10	0.12	0.50	0.80	0.24

Using data from **Table 10.1**, calculate the glider's initial velocity, as it passes through the first light gate.

Initial velocity = ... m/s **[3 marks]**

10.3 Using data from **Table 10.1**, calculate the glider's final velocity, as it passes through the second light gate.

Final velocity = ... m/s **[2 marks]**

10.4 Show that the glider's acceleration is about 0.2 m/s²

Select the correct equation from the Physics Equation Sheet.

Show your working.

[3 marks]

Question 10 continues on the next page

10.5 The student takes more measurements to calculate the glider's acceleration for other values of attached weight.

Figure 10.2 shows the student's graph of the experimental results.

Figure 10.2

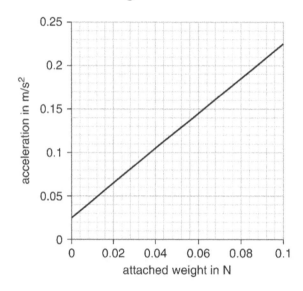

The student expected the results to show that the glider's acceleration is **directly proportional** to the attached weight.

Explain why the graph does **not** confirm what the student was expecting.

....

....

....

.... **[2 marks]**

11 When a car driver becomes aware of a hazard ahead, the distance that the car travels before it stops is known as the **stopping distance**. This depends on the car's speed.

11.1 Explain what is meant in this scenario by

- the **thinking distance** and
- the **braking distance**

and how they relate to the stopping distance.

Describe the effect of **three** factors, other than speed, that can affect the size of **each** of these two distances.

[6 marks]

Question 11 continues on the next page

11.2 **Figure 11.1** shows how thinking distance and braking distance each depend on a car's speed.

Figure 11.1

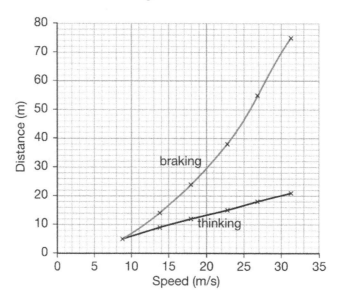

Use **Figure 11.1** to compare the way that thinking distance and braking distance are affected by speed.

Include **at least one similarity** and **at least one difference**.

....

....

....

.... **[3 marks]**

11.3 When a car's brakes are applied, the braking force does work in transferring the car's kinetic energy to thermal energy.

A typical car moving at a speed of 20 m/s has about 200 000 J of kinetic energy.

Estimate the average braking force required to stop the car in an emergency.

Select the required data from **Figure 11.1**

Show your working.

Average braking force ≈ _____ N **[3 marks]**

END OF QUESTIONS

Physics Equation Sheet

Equation Number	Word Equation	Symbol Equation
1	pressure due to a column of liquid = height of column × density of liquid × gravitational field strength	$p = h\,\rho\,g$
2	(final velocity)² – (initial velocity)² = 2 × acceleration × distance	$v^2 - u^2 = 2\,a\,s$
3	force = $\dfrac{\text{change in momentum}}{\text{time taken}}$	$F = \dfrac{m\Delta v}{\Delta t}$
4	elastic potential energy = 0.5 × spring constant × (extension)²	$E_e = \dfrac{1}{2}\,ke^2$
5	change in thermal energy = mass × specific heat capacity × temperature change	$\Delta E = m\,c\,\Delta\theta$
6	period = $\dfrac{1}{\text{frequency}}$	
7	magnification = $\dfrac{\text{image height}}{\text{object height}}$	
8	force on a conductor (at right-angles to a magnetic field) carrying a current = magnetic flux density × current × length	$F = B\,I\,l$
9	thermal energy for a change of state = mass × specific latent heat	$E = m\,L$
10	$\dfrac{\text{potential difference across primary coil}}{\text{potential difference across secondary coil}} =$ $\dfrac{\text{number of turns in primary coil}}{\text{number of turns in seconday coil}}$	$\dfrac{V_p}{V_s} = \dfrac{n_p}{n_s}$
11	potential difference across primary coil × current in primary coil = potential difference across secondary coil × current in secondary coil	$V_p I_p = V_s I_s$
12	For gases: pressure × volume = constant	$pV = \text{constant}$

Answers

Set A – Paper 1

Question	Answer(s)	Extra info	Mark(s)	AO/Spec ref.
01.1	beta		1	AO1 4.4.2.1
01.2	(Radiation with a high ionising power) produces a large number of ions (when the radiation collides with atoms)		1	AO1 4.4.2.1
	along each cm of its path (accept in a given distance).		1	
	Alpha radiation has a short range in the human body (accept doesn't pass through skin/flesh)		1	
01.3	Gamma radiation (easily) passes through the human body		1	AO1 4.4.3.3
01.4	6 hours		1	AO1 4.4.3.3
	The half-life has to be long enough so that the procedure can be completed.		1	
	Half-life has to be short enough so that the patient is not radioactive for a long period of time.		1	
02.1	**Level 2:** A detailed and coherent plan covering all the major steps is provided. The steps are presented in a logical order that could be followed by another person to obtain valid results.	3–4	4	AO1 4.2.1.3
	Level 1: Simple statements relating to relevant apparatus or steps are made but may not follow a logical sequence. The plan would not enable another person to obtain valid results.	1–2		
	No relevant content		0	
	Indicative content: • measure the length of wire between the crocodile clips • using a metre rule • close the switch • record the reading on the ammeter • record the reading on the voltmeter • open switch to stop the wire overheating • divide the voltmeter reading by the ammeter reading to determine the wire's resistance • repeat measurement to improve accuracy/minimise errors • repeat for different lengths of wire • plot a graph of resistance against length			
02.2	systematic error (accept zero error)		1	AO3 4.2.1.3 4.2.1.4
02.3	deduct 1 mm from each length measurement		1	AO3 4.2.1.3 4.2.1.4
02.4	straight line, positive gradient, through the origin		1	AO1 4.2.1.3 4.2.1.4
02.5	resistance decreases as the thickness increases Accept any other conclusion consistent with the pattern shown by the graph, such as doubling thickness reduces resistance to $\frac{1}{4}$		1	AO3 4.2.1.3
02.6	accept value in the range 1.6–2.5 (Ω)		1	AO3 4.2.1.3
03.1	$(\Delta E = m\, c\, \Delta\theta)$ $\Delta E = 1 \times 4200 \times 80$ thermal energy transferred $= 336\,000$ (J)	1 mark for substitution into correct equation 1 mark for answer correct answer with no working shown = 2 marks	2	AO2 4.1.1.3
03.2	energy transferred = power × time	accept power = energy transferred / time	1	AO1 4.2.4.2
03.3	thermal energy transferred = 3000 × 120 = 360 000 (J)	1 mark for substitution 1 mark for answer correct answer with no working shown = 2 marks	2	AO2 4.2.4.2
03.4	either: efficiency = $\frac{\text{(useful output energy transfer)}}{\text{(total input energy transfer)}}$ or: efficiency = $\frac{\text{useful power output}}{\text{total power input}}$		1	AO1 4.1.2.2
03.5	efficiency = $\frac{336000}{360000} \times 100$ efficiency = 93(%)	1 mark for substitution 1 mark for answer Correct answer with no working shown = 2 marks Allow error carried forward from 03.2 and 03.3 1 additional mark if answer given to 2 significant figures	2 1	AO2 4.1.2.2
03.6	(Thermal) energy is transferred to the body of the kettle.		1	AO1 4.1.2.1

Question	Answer(s)	Extra info	Mark(s)	AO/Spec ref.
04.1	An energy source that can be replenished / will not run out.	or wtte	1	**AO1** 4.1.3
04.2	**Level 3:** A coherent and detailed account comparing wind power and nuclear power in terms of both reliability and environmental effects.	5–6	6	**AO3** 4.1.3
	Level 2: A clear account with some valid comparisons of reliability and environmental effect.	3–4		
	Level 1: Some relevant comments regarding reliability and environmental effects but comparisons may not be made. The descriptions are vague and lack sufficient detail.	1–2		
	No relevant content		0	
	Indicative content **Wind power:** • renewable / doesn't run out • not reliable / predictable: only supplies energy when it is windy • usually windy somewhere in the UK • does not cause (atmospheric) pollution • no greenhouse gas emissions/does not contribute to climate change • noise disturbance may be an issue • possible hazard to birds • visual impact of turbines may be an issue **Nuclear power:** • not renewable / will run out • reliable: supplies energy continuously/ no disruption to the supply • not dependent on the weather • no greenhouse gas emissions/does not contribute to climate change • produces radioactive waste which may be hazardous for hundreds of years • accidents can lead to the emission of radioactive material into the environment			
05.1	Accept either 10^{-9} or 10^{-10} (m)		1	**AO1** 4.4.1.1

Question	Answer(s)	Extra info	Mark(s)	AO/Spec ref.
05.2	That a very small percentage are deflected by large angles could not be explained by plum pudding model / Needed to change model so that the positive charge / most of the mass is in a nucleus	1 mark	2	**AO3** 4.4.1.3
	Any 3 of: Both models have positive (and negative charge) present in the atom Positive charge is distributed throughout the atom in the plum pudding model but is contained within the central nucleus in the nuclear model Repulsion occurs between the alpha particles and the nucleus because they are both positively charged Most of the atom must be empty space. Deflected alpha particles must be hitting a small concentrated region of positive charge.	1 mark 1 mark each for any two of the three statements	2	**AO1** 4.4.1.3
05.3	79 protons in the nucleus		1	**AO1**
	118 neutrons in the nucleus		1	4.4.1.1
	79 electrons orbiting (surrounding) the nucleus		1	4.4.1.2
	at different distances or in different energy levels / shells		1	
06.1	cosmic rays / rocks / construction materials / food and drink	1 mark for any one source	1	**AO1** 4.4.3.1
06.2	the radon gas enters the human body when a person breathes in.		1	**AO1** 4.4.2.1
	the alpha particles emitted (by the radon) produce a lot of ionisation (accept the short range of alphas means all are absorbed by the body)		1	
	which is very damaging to the cells / the body / human tissue		1	

Question	Answer(s)	Extra info	Mark(s)	AO/Spec ref.
06.3	number of times greater = 5.3		1	**AO3** 4.4.3.1
06.4	time for activity to fall by half e.g. from 2000 to 1000: 3.8 days second set of values, e.g. 1000 to 500: 7.6 – 3.8 = 3.8 days average = 3.8 days half-life = 3.8 (days)	1 mark for working shown on graph 1 mark for obtaining 2 or more values and taking an average 1 mark for correct half-life allow maximum of 1 mark for correct answer with no working shown	3	**AO3** 4.4.2.3
06.5	at least 4 half-lives would have to pass accept 14, 15 or 16 days	1 mark 1 mark Allow error carried forward from 06.4 for half-life value	2	**AO2** 4.4.2.3
06.6	$^{222}_{86}Rn \rightarrow\ ^{218}_{84}Po + ^{4}_{2}He$	1 mark each for each correctly substituted number	2	**AO2** 4.4.2.2
07.1	National Grid		1	**AO1** 4.2.4.3
07.2	(potential difference) continually changes direction / reverses direction		1	**AO1** 4.2.3.1
07.3	a person touching the casing could be electrocuted / current could pass through them (to earth)		1 1	**AO1** 4.2.3.2
07.4	earth (wire)	allow 'green and yellow striped one' or wtte	1	**AO1** 4.2.3.2
07.5	$(P = V\,I)$ $920 = 230 \times I$ $I = \dfrac{920}{230}$ current = 4.0 (A) (accept 4)	1 mark for substitution into correct equation 1 mark for rearranging 1 mark for answer correct answer with no working shown = 3 marks	3	**AO2** 4.2.4.1
08.1	$(V = I\,R)$ $3.0 = I \times 100$ $I = \dfrac{3.0}{100}$ current = 0.030 (A) (accept 0.03)	1 mark for substitution into correct equation 1 mark for rearranging 1 mark for answer correct answer with no working shown = 3 marks	3	**AO2** 4.2.1.3

Question	Answer(s)	Extra info	Mark(s)	AO/Spec ref.
08.2	5 mins = 300 s $(Q = I\,t)$ $Q = 0.030 \times 300$ charge = 9.0 (C) (accept 9)	1 mark for correct unit conversion 1 mark for substitution into correct equation 1 mark for evaluation correct answer with no working shown = 3 marks	3	**AO2** 4.2.1.2
08.3	(energy transferred = $Q\,V$) energy transferred = 9.0×3.0 energy transferred = 27 (J)	1 mark for substitution into correct equation 1 mark for answer correct answer with no working shown = 2 marks	2	**AO2** 4.2.4.2
08.4	The potential difference across each bulb has the same value. The bulbs are connected in parallel.	1 mark for each correct statement ticked maximum 2 boxes ticked	2	**AO1** 4.2.2
08.5	The bulbs are connected in series. The current through each bulb has the same value.	1 mark for each correct statement ticked maximum 2 boxes ticked	2	**AO1** 4.2.2

Question	Answer(s)		Extra info	Mark(s)	AO/Spec ref.
09.1	**Level 3:** Coherent and detailed account that could be followed to generate data from which a valid comparison of the insulating materials can be made. Reference made to variables that must be the same for each material tested.	5–6		6	**AO2** 4.1.2.1
	Level 2: Following the account would enable data to be produced that could enable a comparison of the thermal properties of the materials to be made although the account may lack detail.	3–4			
	Level 1: Some relevant content but may not generate data which would enable a fair comparison of the materials. There may be no indication of how to use equipment, control variables or use measurements.	1–2			
	No relevant content	0			
	Indicative content: • pack the material to be tested in the space between the two beakers • the gap between the beaker is constant so the thickness of material is the same for all the materials tested • pour a specific volume of hot water into the inner beaker • put the lid on the beaker • use a stop clock to measure the time for the temperature to drop by a specific amount e.g. 80°C to 60°C • repeat for each material using the same volume of water and the same temperature drop • both the volume of water and the specific temperature drop must be the same for each material tested • compare the time measurements • the material which took the longest time for its temperature to drop by the specified amount is the best insulator				
09.2	cotton wool			1	**AO3** 4.1.2.1

Question	Answer(s)		Extra info	Mark(s)	AO/Spec ref.
09.3	either: the energy / rate of energy conducted is inversely proportional to thickness or: doubling the wall thickness halves the transfer of (thermal) energy / halves the rate of transfer		1 mark for either statement	1	**AO3** 4.1.2.1
	data quoted from two points on the graph where one point corresponds to double the thickness of the other, to support the conclusion above		1 mark each for the two suitable data sets	2	
10.1	random / haphazard/in all directions			1	**AO1** 4.3.3.1
10.2	(air) molecules collide with the wall			1	**AO1** 4.3.3.1
10.3	air molecules move faster		1 mark	2	**AO1** 4.3.3.1
	either: molecules exert a larger force (on the walls of the container) or: molecules hit walls more frequently		1 mark for either statement		
10.4	$p_1V_1 = p_2V_2$ $1.0 \times 10^5 \times 2.4 \times 10^{-3}$ $= p \times 3.2 \times 10^{-3}$ $p = \dfrac{1.0 \times 10^5 \times 2.4 \times 10^{-3}}{3.2 \times 10^{-3}}$ new gas pressure = 7.5×10^4 (Pa)		1 mark for substitution into correct equation 1 mark for rearranging 1 mark for answer correct answer with no working shown = 3 marks	3	**AO2** 4.3.3.2

10.5	Quantity	Increases	Decreases	Doesn't change		AO2 4.1.2.2
	Internal energy of the molecules	✓			1	
	Average molecule speed	✓			1	
	Average separation of the molecules		✓		1	

Question	Answer(s)	Extra info	Mark(s)	AO/Spec ref.
11.1	gravitational potential energy = $100 \times 10 \times 10$ = 10 000 (J) 50% of g.p.e. becomes kinetic energy $5000 = \frac{1}{2} \times 100 \times v^2$ speed = $\sqrt{\frac{2 \times 5000}{100}}$ speed = 10 m/s	1 mark for substitution into correct equation 1 mark for calculation of g.p.e. 1 mark for substitution into correct equation for k.e. 1 mark for rearranging for speed 1 mark for answer correct answer with no working shown = 5 marks	5	AO2 4.1.1.2

Set A – Paper 2

Question	Answer(s)	Extra info	Mark(s)	AO/Spec ref.
01.1	either: oscillations are parallel to the direction the wave travels or: has areas of compression and rarefaction	1 mark for either statement	1	AO1 4.6.1.1
01.2	sound travels at different speeds through different materials sound travels faster through liquids than gases sound travels faster through solids than liquids	Accept any other conclusion consistent with the data. maximum 3 marks	1 1 1	AO3 4.6.1.4
01.3	speed = frequency × wavelength	accept $v = f\lambda$	1	AO1 4.6.1.2
01.4	$4000 = 500 \times$ wavelength wavelength = $\frac{4000}{500}$ wavelength = 8 (m)	1 mark for substitution 1 mark for rearranging 1 mark for answer correct answer with no working shown = 3 marks	3	AO2 4.6.1.2
01.5	20 Hz to 20 kHz	only one box ticked	1	AO1 4.6.1.4

Question	Answer(s)	Extra info	Mark(s)	AO/Spec ref.
01.6	one of: medical imaging industrial imaging echo sounding	1 mark allow any other suitable application	1	AO1 4.6.1.5
02.1	The resultant force on a stationary object is zero. The resultant force on an object moving at a steady speed is zero.	1 mark each only two boxes ticked	2	AO1 4.5.6.2.1
02.2	rolling resistance is not affected by the speed of the cyclist. air resistance increases with speed the rate at which the air resistance increases with speed gets greater at higher speeds		1 1 1	AO3 4.5.6.2
02.3	rolling resistance = 2 N air resistance = 7.5 N (accept 7 to 8 N) total resistive force = 9.5 (N) (accept 9 to 10)	1 mark 1 mark 1 mark correct answer with no working shown = 3 marks	3	AO2 4.5.6.2
02.4	work done = force × distance moved (in line of action of force)	accept $W = F\,s$ or $W = F\,d$	1	AO1 4.5.2
02.5	work done = 9.5 × 200 work done = 1900 (accept 1800 to 2000) unit: accept either J or N m	1 mark for substitution 1 mark for answer correct answer with no working shown = 2 marks allow error carried forward from 02.3 1 mark for correct unit	2 1	AO2 4.5.2, 4.5.6.2.1 AO1 4.5.2
02.6	force = mass × acceleration	accept $F = ma$	1	AO1 4.5.6.2.2
02.7	$F = 70 \times 2$ resultant force = 140 (N)	1 mark for substitution 1 mark for answer correct answer with no working shown = 2 marks	2	AO2 4.5.6.2.2

Question	Answer(s)	Extra info	Mark(s)	AO/Spec ref.
03.1	**Level 2:** A clear method referring specifically to the apparatus shown that would obtain valid results. At least one reference to minimising errors needed to gain the maximum mark.	3–4	4	**AO2** 4.5.3
	Level 1: A basic method that would obtain an extension measurement is given but may not refer specifically to the apparatus shown.	1–2		
	No relevant content	0		

	Indicative content:
	• with no weight attached, the metre rule reading in line with the pointer is recorded
	• a standard / known weight is attached to the spring
	• the metre rule reading in line with the pointer is again recorded.
	• the extension is the difference between the two readings
	• to minimise errors:
	  ◦ view the pointer from the same horizontal level
	  ◦ take repeat readings and average			

03.2	extension is directly proportional to the (stretching) force either: spring is not stretched beyond its limit of proportionality or: spring is behaving elastically / not inelastically deformed	1 mark 1 mark for either statement Accept alternative wording	2	**AO3** 4.5.3
03.3	force = spring constant × extension	accept $F = k\,e$	1	**AO1** 4.5.3
03.4	correct data taken from graph to determine spring constant use of $F = k\,e$ $k = F/e$ $k = 50$ N/m	1 mark 1 mark for substitution 1 mark for rearrangement 1 mark for correct answer	4	**AO2** 4.5.3

Question	Answer(s)	Extra info	Mark(s)	AO/Spec ref.
04.1	(moment = force × distance) 18 = force × 3.0 force = $\frac{18}{3.0}$ force = 6.0 (N) (accept 6)	1 mark for substitution into correct equation 1 mark for rearranging and answer correct answer with no working 2 marks	2	**AO2** 4.5.4
04.2	(anticlockwise moment = clockwise moment) 400 × 0.40 = F × 1.7 force = 94 N	1 mark for substitution into correct equation 1 mark for answer correct answer with no working 2 marks additional 1 mark if correct answer given to 2 s.f.	2 1	**AO2** 4.5.4
05.1	(momentum = 60 × 10) momentum = 600 (kg m/s)	1 mark for the correct answer	1	**AO2** 4.5.7.1
05.2	(force = $\frac{\text{change of momentum}}{\text{time}}$) force = $\frac{(600-0)}{0.1}$ force = 6000 N	1 mark for substitution into correct equation 1 mark for answer correct answer with no working 2 marks allow error carried forward from 05.1	2	**AO2** 4.5.7.3
05.3	**Level 2:** Coherent explanation considering changes in impact time and the rate at which the momentum changes.	3–4	4	**AO1** 4.5.7.3
	Level 1: Some relevant statements but may not refer specifically to the rate at which momentum changes.	1–2		
	No relevant content	0		
	Indicative content: • at the point of impact the air bag automatically inflates • when the dummy hits the inflated air bag, the air bag starts to deflate • the air bag deflates as air / gas exits through a hole in the air bag • the effect of the air bag deflating is to bring the dummy to a stop in a longer time than the collision impact time (of 0.1 s)			

Question	Answer(s)	Extra info	Mark(s)	AO/Spec ref.
	• the dummy's momentum change has the same value whether the air bag is present or not • when the air bag is present, the dummy's momentum changes at a slower rate • impact force is equal to the rate of change of momentum • so the impact force is reduced			
06.1	pressure in a liquid increases with depth either: the force pushing the water out of the hole is greater the deeper the water or: there is a greater weight of water / liquid above the water nearer the bottom of the can	1 mark 1 mark for either statement accept other correct statement	2	AO1 4.5.5.1.2
06.2	(liquid pressure = $h \rho g$) water pressure = $1000 \times 1030 \times 9.8$ water pressure = 1.0×10^7 (Pa)	1 mark for substitution into correct equation 1 mark for answer correct answer with no working = 2 marks additional 1 mark for answer given to 2 s.f. and in standard form	2 1	AO2 4.5.5.1.2
06.3	as height (above sea level) increases, atmospheric pressure decreases		1	AO3 4.5.5.2
06.4	no, the student's suggestion is incorrect justification: pressure and height data correctly selected for two different heights.	1 mark 2 marks	3	AO3 4.5.5.2
07.1	independent variable: angle of incidence dependent variable: angle of refraction control variable: material (of the transparent block) (or any other appropriate control variable)		1 1 1	AO3 4.6.2.2

Question	Answer(s)	Extra info	Mark(s)	AO/Spec ref.
07.2	normal	1 mark for refracted ray and for emerging ray 1 mark for angles towards and away from normal correct in each case	2	AO1 4.6.2.2
07.3	both missing data points correctly plotted best fitting curve passing within ½ small square of each point	1 mark for both points correctly plotted to within ½ small square 1 mark	2	AO2 4.6.2.2
07.4	angle of refraction increases as the angle of incidence increases but not in direct proportion angle of refraction tends towards a limiting value (or any other conclusion consistent with the graph)		1 1	AO3 4.6.2.2
07.5	incident ray, wavefront, air, transparent block, refracted ray	four wavefronts drawn parallel to each other in direction shown for 1 mark wavefronts equally spaced for 1 mark wavefronts closer together than incident wavefronts for 1 mark	3	AO1 4.6.2.2
07.6	(wavelength) decreases		1	AO1 4.6.2.2
07.7	(wave) speed decreases because $v = f\lambda$ shows that $v \propto \lambda$		1 1	AO1 4.6.2.2
08.1	move magnet downwards (or upwards) into the coil / cardboard tube move coil / cardboard tube downwards (or upwards) around / over the magnet		1 1	AO1 4.7.3.1
08.2	rotating the handle makes the coil move / rotate so the coil is moving relative to the magnetic field		1 1	AO1 4.7.3.2
08.3	positive and negative peaks / values of potential difference		1	AO3 4.7.3.2
08.4	0.5 (s)		1	AO3 4.7.3.2
08.5	2.0 (V) (accept 2)		1	AO3 4.7.3.2

Question	Answer(s)	Extra info	Mark(s)	AO/Spec ref.
08.6	maximum potential difference would be greater	1 mark	2	AO1 4.7.3.1 4.7.3.2
	either: one cycle would take a smaller time / time between peaks would be smaller or: frequency would be greater	1 mark		
09.1	arrows on (at least two) field lines showing direction from left to right	1 mark	1	AO1 4.7.1.2
09.2		1 mark for arrow upwards as shown	1	AO2 4.7.2.2
09.3	($F = B I l$) F = 0.20 × 3.2 × 0.050 force = 0.032 (N)	1 mark for substitution into correct equation 1 mark for answer correct answer with no working 2 marks	2	AO2 4.7.2.2
09.4	(magnetic) force on one side of the coil is up	1 mark	3	AO1 4.7.2.3
	(magnetic) force on the other side of the coil is down	1 mark		
	creating a moment / turning effect	1 mark		

Question	Answer(s)	Extra info	Mark(s)	AO/Spec ref.
10.1	**Level 3**: Coherent description of all major stages in the correct sequence. Similarity in initial stages up to main sequence highlighted with clear distinction between later stages. The response makes logical links between clearly identified relevant points.	5–6	6	AO1 4.8.1.1 4.8.1.2
	Level 2: Coherent description of all major stages. Some details may be missing.	3–4		
	Level 1: Simple, relevant statements are made. The response may fail to make logical links between the points raised.	1–2		
	No relevant content	0		

Indicative content:

- birth to main sequence same stages for all stars
- all stars are born in gas / dust cloud
- gravity compresses the gas/dust to form a protostar
- protostar gets hotter
- (nuclear) fusion of hydrogen starts
- lots of energy is released
- while there is plenty of hydrogen to fuse the star is stable and is classed as a main sequence star
- main sequence phase ends when run out of fuel / hydrogen to fuse
- a star like the Sun is a main sequence star for much longer than a much more massive star
- a star like the Sun expands to becomes a red giant
- a much more massive star expands much more to become a red supergiant
- the red giant blows away outer layers leaving its core as a small white dwarf
- the red supergiant undergoes a massive explosion called a supernova leaving its core as either a neutron star or a black hole
- high mass stars end with huge explosions of their outer layers / supernovae, whereas smaller mass stars do not have supernovae
- high mass stars go on to form black holes or neutron stars whereas low mass stars form white / black dwarfs

Question	Answer(s)	Extra info	Mark(s)	AO/Spec ref.
11.1	gradient = $\frac{8}{10}$ acceleration = 0.8 (m/s²)	1 mark for correct data taken from graph to determine gradient 1 mark for answer	2	**AO2** 4.5.6.1.5
11.2	indication that the student has interpreted the enclosed area as the distance travelled area = (5 × 8) + (8 × 10) distance travelled = 120 m average speed = $\frac{120}{20}$ average speed = 6.0 m/s (accept 6)	1 mark 1 mark for calculation of distance travelled 1 mark for substitution into $s = vt$ and rearranging 1 mark for calculation of average speed correct answer with no working shown = 4 marks	4	**AO2** 4.5.6.1.5

Question	Answer(s)	Extra info	Mark(s)	AO/Spec ref.
01.1	**Level 2:** Coherent account detailing the difference and similarities of solids, liquids and gases. Both molecule motion and arrangement included.	3–4	4	AO1 4.3.1.1
	Level 1: Relevant comments comparing solids and liquids or liquids and gases but comparisons may not be made. Both molecule motion and arrangement for maximum mark.	1–2		
	No relevant content		0	
	Indicative content: Molecules in solid and liquid much closer than in gases Molecules in liquid (slightly) further apart than in solid Molecules in solid in a lattice / ordered arrangement In liquid, arrangement of molecules is less ordered Molecules in solid vibrate about a fixed position Molecules in solid are joined together Molecules in a liquid and gas move around, passing each other Molecules in a liquid and gas move randomly / in all directions			
01.2	Total kinetic energy and potential energy of all the atoms / molecules / particles in the material	1 mark for kinetic energy 1 mark for potential energy 1 mark for 'total' and/or 'all the atoms/ molecules'	3	AO1 4.3.2.1
01.3	The water temperature is increased The water is changed to steam at 100°C	Only two boxes ticked	1 1	AO1 4.3.2.1

Question	Answer(s)	Extra info	Mark(s)	AO/Spec ref.
02.1	**Level 2:** A coherent description of the steps required to demonstrate: – repulsion between like charges – attraction between unlike charges. For the maximum mark, the plan should include the initial step involving charging by friction	3–4	4	AO2 4.2.5.1
	Level 1: A clear description of steps that demonstrate: EITHER: repulsion between like charges OR attraction between unlike charges. For the maximum mark, the plan should include the initial step involving charging by friction	1–2		
	No relevant content		0	
	Indicative content: The rods can be charged by rubbing with a cloth Hold the charged rod close to the suspended rods A charged acetate rod repels a charged suspended acetate rod A charged polythene rod repels a charged suspended polythene rod A charged polythene rod attracts a charged suspended acetate rod A charged acetate rod attracts a charged suspended polyethene rod			
02.2	At least 4 radial field lines from the sphere's outer surface, evenly spaced Arrows on the radial lines point towards the sphere.		1 1	AO1 4.2.5.2
02.3	A repulsive force getting bigger	Only one box ticked	1	AO1 4.2.5.2
03.1	Light dependent resistor (accept LDR)		1	AO1 4.2.1.1
03.2	Total resistance = 500 (Ω)		1	AO2 4.2.2
03.3	Potential difference = current × resistance	Accept $V = I\,R$	1	AO1 4.2.1.3

Question	Answer(s)	Extra info	Mark(s)	AO/Spec ref.
03.4	$12 = I \times 500$ $I = \dfrac{12}{500}$ Ammeter reading = 0.024 (A)	1 mark for substitution 1 mark for rearranging 1 mark for answer Correct answer with no working shown = 3 marks Allow ecf from 03.2	3	AO2 4.2.1.3
03.5	Ammeter reading would decrease Because graph shows that circuit resistance increases in the dark		1 1	AO1 4.2.1.3 AO3 4.2.1.4
04.1	Ammeter in series with wire Variable resistor in correct position to enable the current through the wire to be changed. Voltmeter in correct position 	Allow ammeter and variable resistor to be in swapped places, or next to each other, as long as they are in series	1 1 1	AO1 4.2.1.4
04.2	Current is directly proportional to potential difference Yes (wire is an ohmic conductor)		1 1	AO3 4.2.1.4 AO1 4.2.1.4
04.3	Curve through origin as shown Negative section of line shown 		1 1	AO1 4.2.1.4
04.4	As the current increases, the filament gets hotter. Filament resistance increases as its temperature increases		1 1	AO1 4.2.1.4

Question	Answer(s)	Extra info	Mark(s)	AO/Spec ref.
05.1	Either: Alpha particles are not very penetrating Or: Alpha particles have low penetrating power And: Either: So alpha particles would not be able to pass out through the patient's body Or: So alpha particles could not be detected outside the patient's body	1 mark for either statement 1 mark for either statement	2	AO1 4.4.2.1 4.4.3.3
05.2	It allows sufficient time to conduct the investigation (before it has all decayed) Patient is not exposed to radiation for too long a time		1 1	AO1 4.4.3.3
05.3	Patient's body remains radioactive/contaminated (for a significant period of time) Gamma (and beta) radiation will be emitted from the patient and could reach other people. This radiation could harm/would be a hazard to other people		1 1 1	AO1 4.4.3.3 4.4.2.4
06.1	$(E_p = m\,g\,h)$ $= 0.05 \times 10 \times 0.42$ Gain in gravitational potential energy = 0.21(J)	1 mark for substitution into correct equation 1 mark for answer Correct answer with no working shown = 2 marks	2	AO2 4.1.1.2
06.2	$(E_k = \dfrac{1}{2}\,m\,v^2)$ $E_k = \dfrac{1}{2} \times 0.05 \times 2.0^2$ $= 0.1$ J Kinetic energy (accept 0.1)	1 mark for substitution into correct equation 1 mark for answer Correct answer with no working shown = 2 marks	2	AO2 4.1.1.2
06.3	Energy is dissipated / transferred to the surroundings / as thermal energy / sound energy		1	AO1 4.1.2.1

Question	Answer(s)	Extra info	Mark(s)	AO/Spec ref.
07.1	Tangent drawn on curve at time 80s, working shows gradient data taken from the graph using a large triangle Gradient calculated Allow gradient in range 0.35 to 0.6 °C/s	1 mark for data extraction 1 mark for gradient in the range given	2	AO2 4.1.2.1
07.2	As the water gets hotter its temperature rise per second decreases. The gradient of the graph line decreases as the water temperature rises.		1 1	AO3 4.1.2.1
07.3	(The rate of dissipation of thermal energy to the surroundings) increases as the water temperature rises.		1	AO3 4.1.2.1
07.4	Polypropylene The lower the thermal conductivity, the lower the rate of energy transfer.		1 1	AO3 4.1.2.1 AO1 4.1.2.1
08.1	**Level 3:** A coherent plan covering all steps presented in a logical order detailing any additional apparatus used. The plan could be followed by another person to obtain a valid result for density. Reference made to minimising errors.	5–6	6	AO2 4.3.1.1
	Level 2: A clear plan covering all major experiment steps presented in a logical order detailing any additional apparatus used. The plan could be followed by another person to obtain valid results for the mass and volume of the pebble. At least one valid suggestion about reducing errors is made, with reasons.	3–4		
	Level 1: Some relevant statements but the plan could not be followed by another person to obtain valid results. There may be no indication of how to use equipment, use measurements or reduce errors.	1–2		
	No relevant content	0		
	Indicative content: Beaker and additional measuring cylinder required Fill the displacement can with water and allow the excess to drain into a beaker.			

Question	Answer(s)	Extra info	Mark(s)	AO/Spec ref.
	Place the measuring cylinder under the spout of the displacement can. Lower the pebble into the can using the thread attached. Measure the volume of water in the measuring cylinder. The volume of displaced water is equal to the volume of the pebble. Repeat the process using a dry measuring cylinder of the same size. Calculate an average value for the volume of the pebble. Measure the mass of the (dry) pebble using a balance. Reference to avoiding systematic errors (e.g. reading the measuring cylinder at eye level or taking account of the meniscus, reason pebble is weighed while dry or ensuring the balance is zeroed) Calculate the density of the pebble using $\rho = \dfrac{m}{v}$			
08.2	Record the volume reading of the water in the measuring cylinder Lower the pebble into the measuring cylinder and record new volume Subtract the volume values to get the volume of the pebble		1 1 1	AO2 4.3.1.1
08.3	The size of each graduation in the larger measuring cylinder is bigger than for the smaller measuring cylinder So the volume measurement using the larger measuring cylinder would be less accurate than the method using the displacement can.		1 1	AO3 4.3.1.1
09.1	At least one of the free neutrons is absorbed by another uranium nucleus causing the uranium nucleus to undergo fission releasing more neutrons which go on to cause more fission		1 1 1	AO1 4.4.4.1
09.2	Any number in the range 93–97 Any number in the range 135–139		1 1	AO3 4.4.4.1
09.3	38 protons 52 neutrons		1 1	AO1 4.4.1.2

Question	Answer(s)	Extra info	Mark(s)	AO/Spec ref.
09.4	$^{90}_{38}Sr \rightarrow ^{90}_{39}Y + ^{0}_{-1}e$	1 mark for both correct numbers for yttrium 1 mark for both correct numbers for the beta particle	2	AO2 4.4.2.2
09.5	$\frac{1}{16}$		1	AO2 4.4.2.3
09.6	Alpha particles (from the uranium) only travel a few cm in air/are not very penetrating Beta particles (from the fission fragments) can travel several metres in air/are more penetrating than alpha particles		1 1	AO1 4.4.2.1
09.7	Caesium-137 Krypton-85		1 1	AO3 4.4.3.2
10.1	Material regains its original properties if change is reversed		1	AO1 4.3.1.2
10.2	40 (°C)		1	AO3 4.3.2.3
10.3	10 (minutes)		1	AO3 4.3.2.3
10.4	Energy supplied by heater = 50 × 10 × 60 = 30 000 (J) 30 000 = 0.10 × L $L = \frac{30000}{0.10}$ Specific latent heat of fusion = 300 000 (J/kg)	1 mark for substitution into correct equation 1 mark for calculation of energy supplied Allow ecf from 10.3 1 mark for substitution into correct equation 1 mark for rearranging 1 mark for answer Allow ecf from calculation of energy supplied Correct answer with no working shown = 5 marks	5	AO2 4.1.1.4

Question	Answer(s)	Extra info	Mark(s)	AO/Spec ref.
10.5	Specific heat capacity in solid state is **larger** than in the liquid state Temperature rise in the solid state slower/lower rate than in the liquid state		1 1	AO3 4.3.2.2
11.1	$(V = IR)$ $9 = I \times 15$ $I = \frac{9}{15}$ Current ≈ 0.6 (A)	1 mark for substitution into correct equation 1 mark for rearranging 1 mark for answer Correct answer with no working shown = 3 marks Do not accept 0.60 A	3	AO2 4.2.1.3
11.2	Ammeter Y Its maximum current exceeds current in circuit Best (smallest) resolution in that current range / can measure smaller difference in current	If explanation is fully correct but ammeter chosen is wrong because of incorrect current calculated in 11.1, award 3 marks	1 1 1	AO3 4.2.1.3
11.3	(power = potential difference × current) $P = 8.0 \times 0.55$ Power = 4.4 W (energy transferred = power × time) Energy supplied = 4.4 × 500 = 2200 J	1 mark for substitution into correct equation to calculate the power of the heater 1 mark for calculation of power 1 mark for substitution into correct equation to calculate energy supplied Correct answer with no working shown = 3 marks	3	AO2 4.2.4.1 and 4.2.4.2

Question	Answer(s)	Extra info	Mark(s)	AO/Spec ref.
11.4	$2200 = 0.50 \times c \times (30.1 - 20.1)$ $c = \dfrac{2200}{0.50 \times (30.1 - 20.1)}$ Specific heat capacity $= 440$	1 mark for substitution into correct equation 1 mark for rearranging 1 mark for answer Correct answer with no working shown = 3 marks Allow ecf from 11.3	3	AO2 4.1.1.3
	Unit: J/kg°C	1 mark for unit	1	AO1 4.1.1.3

Set B – Paper 2

Question	Answer(s)	Extra info	Mark(s)	AO/Spec ref.
01.1	Refraction		1	AO1 4.6.2.2
01.2	Two rays with arrows passing through the lens as shown below. convex lens Extrapolation of rays as dashed or dotted lines to show formation of an image (I) Image labelled (accept 'I' as the label)	1 mark for each ray 1 mark 1 mark	4	AO1 4.6.2.5
01.3	Can be either real or virtual Can be either upright or upside down	1 mark each No more than two boxes ticked	2	AO1 4.6.2.5
01.4	Always virtual Always upright	1 mark each No more than two boxes ticked	2	AO1 4.6.2.5
02.1	Weight (accept gravity) Normal contact force		1 1	AO1 4.5.1.3 4.5.1.2

Question	Answer(s)	Extra info	Mark(s)	AO/Spec ref.
02.2	C		1	AO3 4.5.6.1.5
02.3	B		1	AO3 4.5.6.1.5
02.4	Up and down arrows drawn, with down arrow larger than the up arrow Up arrow labelled air resistance Down arrow labelled weight (accept gravity) air resistance weight	1 mark 1 mark 1 mark	3	AO2 4.5.1.4
02.5	Weight (accept gravity) Upthrust		1 1	AO1 4.5.1.3 4.5.5.1.2
03.1	Speed $= \dfrac{9.42 \times 10^{11}}{3.15 \times 10^{7}}$ Speed $= 2.99 \times 10^4$ m/s	1 mark for substitution and rearrangement of speed equation 1 mark for evaluation Correct answer with no working shown = 2 marks Additional 1 mark for correct answer given in standard form and to 3 sig figs	2 1	AO2 4.5.6.1.2

Question	Answer(s)	Extra info	Mark(s)	AO/Spec ref.
03.2	Number of times more massive $= \frac{10^{42}}{10^{30}} = 10^{12}$	1 mark for substitution 1 mark for answer Correct answer with no working shown = 2 marks	2	**AO2** 4.8.1.1
03.3	Red giant		1	**AO1** 4.8.1.2
	Massive expansion means the surface / outer layers of the Sun could reach / engulf the Earth		1	
04.1	An increase in wavelength of the light		1	**AO1** 4.8.2
	(as a result) of the distant galaxy receding (moving away from us)		1	
04.2	(in the previous model) the universe was thought to be static	1 mark each for any three correct statements	3	**AO1** 4.8.2
	Observations suggested universe was expanding / everything in the universe was flying apart			
	Observations led to the idea that the universe began from a small (hot and dense) region			
	New model was needed: Big Bang (replaces old model)			
05.1	Radio waves		1	**AO1** 4.6.2.1
05.2	Visible light		1	**AO1** 4.6.2.1
05.3	ultraviolet		1	**AO1** 4.6.2.3
05.4	Infrared		1	**AO1** 4.6.2.4
	Microwaves		1	
	(Either order)			
05.5	X-rays are (mainly) absorbed by bony tissue		1	**AO1** 4.6.2.4
	X-rays (mainly) pass through soft tissue		1	

Question	Answer(s)	Extra info	Mark(s)	AO/Spec ref.
05.6	$(v = f\lambda$ $f = \frac{v}{\lambda})$ frequency $= \frac{3.0 \times 10^8}{2.0 \times 10^{-10}}$	1 mark for rearrangement of and substitution into correct equation	2	**AO2** 4.6.1.2
	Frequency $= 1.5 \times 10^{18}$	1 mark for evaluation Correct answer with no working shown = 2 marks		**AO1** 4.6.1.2
	Unit: Hz	1 mark for unit	1	
05.7	(Figure 6.2 shows that) (electromagnetic) radiation of wavelength 0.1 m (10^{-1}m) is not absorbed by the Earth's atmosphere	1 mark	2	**AO3** 4.6.2.2
	all of or 100% of (electromagnetic) radiation of wavelength 100 m (10^2m) is absorbed by the Earth's atmosphere	1 mark		
06.1	Intensity / power / energy radiated (per square cm) increases as the surface temperature increases	1 mark	2	**AO3** 4.6.3.1
	Intensity / power radiated (per square cm) increases more quickly / at greater rate at higher temperatures	1 mark Accept other conclusion consistent with the graph		
06.2	**Level 2:** A coherent set of instructions that would result in a set of data that would enable the infrared emission rates from the different surfaces to be compared fairly. The need for the metal surface temperature as a control variable must have been considered	3–4	4	**AO2** 4.6.3.1 4.6.2.2
	Level 1: Some relevant content but may not be clear how to make a fair comparison of emission rates from the data generated	1–2		
	No relevant content	0		

Question	Answer(s)	Extra info	Mark(s)	AO/Spec ref.
	Indicative content: Position the infrared sensor at a specific distance from one of the container's surfaces Record an infrared sensor reading at a specific temperature (of the water in the container) Repeat the above steps with the infrared sensor pointing at each of the other three surfaces in turn checking the water temperature remains constant. Distance from sensor to container, and the temperature at which the meter reading is taken must be the same for all four vsurfaces			
06.3	Two of: Different surfaces emit different amounts of energy / infrared radiation in a given time (per square cm) A dull surface emits more energy / infrared radiation than a shiny surface of the same colour in a given time (per square cm) A dull metal / aluminium surface emits more infrared radiation than a polished metal / aluminium surface in a given time (per square cm) The dull black surface emits far more infrared radiation (per second, per square cm) / higher intensity of radiation than any other surface tested	Any two for 1 mark each	2	**AO3** 4.6.2.2
06.4	Two of: The infrared radiation (from the hot object) is made up of different wavelengths The amount of energy radiated varies with wavelength There is a continuous range of wavelengths emitted Most energy radiated at a small range of wavelengths	Any two for 1 mark each Accept other conclusion consistent with the graph	2	**AO3** 4.6.2.2

Question	Answer(s)	Extra info	Mark(s)	AO/Spec ref.
07.1	Two of: Distance, speed, mass, work, energy, time (Allow other answers)	1 mark each, maximum 2 marks	2	**AO1** 4.5.1.1 4.5.6.1.1
07.2	Increasing speed or accelerating Gradient is increasing		1 1	**AO3** 4.5.6.1.4
07.3	Attempt to determine gradient at time 3.0 s by drawing a tangent to the curve and forming large triangle Gradient calculated correctly giving speed in the range 6.9 to 7.6 (m/s)	1 mark 1 mark	2	**AO2** 4.5.6.1.4
07.4	average speed = $\frac{\text{total distance}}{\text{time}} = \frac{32}{5.0}$ average speed = 6.4 (m/s)	1 mark for substitution of data from graph into correct equation 1 mark for evaluation Correct answer with no working shown = 2 marks	2	**AO2** 4.5.6.1.2
08.1	Total momentum before (collision) = total momentum after Momentum of the van before the collision is equal to the momentum of the van and the car after the collision	1 mark for basic principle of momentum conservation But 2 marks for conservation of momentum described in the context of the event	2	**AO2** 4.5.7.2

Question	Answer(s)	Extra info	Mark(s)	AO/Spec ref.
08.2	(Momentum = $m\,v$) Momentum = 1000 × 5.0 = 5000	1 mark for substitution and evaluation of van's momentum before the collision	3	**AO2** 4.5.7.2
	5000 = (800 × 4.0) + (1000 × v)	1 mark for substitution into momentum conservation equation and rearranging		
	$v = \dfrac{5000 - 3200}{1000}$			
	Van's velocity immediately after collision = 1.8 m/s forwards	1 mark for evaluation and direction		
09.1	**Level 2:** Coherent, detailed description presented in a logical sequence leading to a current (or pd) being induced in the secondary coil. For the maximum mark the 'step-down' aspect must be described	3–4	4	**AO1** 4.7.3.4
	Level 1: Some relevant content but may not be presented in a logical sequence	1–2		
	No relevant content	0		
	Indicative content: A step-down transformer is used to reduce the potential difference In a step-down transformer, the secondary pd is smaller than the primary pd The current in the primary is a.c. The primary current induces/creates a magnetic field in the iron core. The magnetic field is changing The changing magnetic field induces a current (or pd) in the secondary coil			

Question	Answer(s)	Extra info	Mark(s)	AO/Spec ref.
09.2	$\dfrac{230}{12} = \dfrac{400}{\text{number of turns in secondary coil}}$ Number of turns in secondary coil = 20.9 = 21 to nearest whole number	1 mark for substitution into correct equation and rearranging 1 mark for evaluation Correct answer with no working shown = 2 marks Additional 1 mark for whole number	2 1	**AO2** 4.7.3.4
09.3	($V_s × I_s = V_p × I_p$) 12 × I_s = 230 × 0.20 $I_s = \dfrac{230 × 0.20}{12}$ Secondary current = 3.8 (A)	1 mark for substitution into correct equation and rearrangement 1 mark for evaluation Correct answer with no working shown = 2 marks Additional 1 mark for 2 significant figures	2 1	**AO2** 4.7.3.4
10.1	Independent variable: Weight (attached to string)	1		**AO3** 4.5.6.2.2
	Dependent variable: acceleration	1		
	Control variable: mass (of glider) (accept same glider or same air track set up or any other appropriate control variable)	1		

Question	Answer(s)	Extra info	Mark(s)	AO/Spec ref.
10.2	$speed = \dfrac{\text{length of glider}}{\text{time to pass through first light gate}}$ $speed = \dfrac{0.12}{0.80} = 0.15$ (m/s)	1 mark for correct equation 1 mark for substitution 1 mark for evaluation Correct answer with no working shown = 3 marks	3	**AO2** 4.5.6.1.2
10.3	$speed = \dfrac{\text{length of glider}}{\text{time to pass through second light gate}}$ $speed = \dfrac{0.12}{0.24} = 0.50$ (m/s) (accept 0.5)	1 mark for substitution 1 mark for evaluation Correct answer with no working shown = 2 marks	2	**AO2** 4.5.6.1.2
10.4	$acceleration = \dfrac{(\text{final velocity})^2 - (\text{initial velocity})^2}{(2 \times \text{gate separation})}$ $acceleration = \dfrac{(0.50^2 - 0.15^2)}{(2 \times 0.5)}$ $= 0.2(3)$ m/s^2	1 mark for rearrangement of correctly chosen equation from Equation Sheet 1 mark for substitution 1 mark for evaluation Allow ecf from 10.2 and 10.3	3	**AO2** 4.5.6.1.5
10.5	(For the results to be as expected by the student) the graph should be a straight line passing through the origin Line misses the origin / has a non-zero y-intercept	1 mark 1 mark	2	**AO3** 4.5.6.2.2

Question	Answer(s)	Extra info	Mark(s)	AO/Spec ref.
11.1	**Level 3:** A coherent account explaining both thinking and braking distance with the effect of at least three factors considered for each	5–6	6	**AO1** 4.5.6.3.1 4.5.6.3.2 4.5.6.3.3
	Level 2: A clear account explaining both thinking and braking distance with the effect of two factors considered for each	3–4		
	Level 1: Some relevant comments but lacks detail	1–2		
	No relevant content	0		
	Indicative content: Thinking distance is the distance travelled by the car during the time that the driver is reacting to an emergency Braking distance is the distance travelled whilst the brakes are being applied Thinking distance + braking distance = stopping distance			
	Thinking distance can increase if the driver: • is tired or • has consumed drugs or alcohol or • is distracted by other people in the car or by other events going on outside the car Braking distance can be increased by: • the road surface, for example a wet or icy road, or • poor condition of the tyres or • poor condition of the brakes • the gradient of the road			
11.2	Both thinking distance and braking distance increase with speed	1		**AO3** 4.5.6.3.1
	Thinking distance increases steadily with speed	1		
	But braking distance increases at an increasing rate with speed	1		

Question	Answer(s)	Extra info	Mark(s)	AO/Spec ref.
11.3	Braking distance = 30 (m) (accept 29 to 31) ($W = F\,s$) $200\,000 = F \times 30$ Average braking force = 6667 (N) (accept 6500 to 6900)	1 mark for correct braking distance extracted from graph 1 mark for substitution into equation for work done 1 mark for evaluation	3	**AO2** 4.5.6.3.4 4.5.2

BLANK PAGE

BLANK PAGE

BLANK PAGE